Kyle Kramer's ʃ ... olic spirituality, a voice that ... ul energy and
the wisdom of tɧ ... lf and God on
a small farm in ʃ ... s and pains of
a life that is at o ... ned. He man-
ages to combine ... ncourages the
quest for a simpler life and reminds us that simpler does not mean easier.

Luke Timothy Johnson
Author of *The Creed: What Christians Believe and Why It Matters*

Unlike many who extol the virtues of sustainable living for political or intellectual reasons, Kramer speaks gently here, making his argument with spiritual candor and a kind of humble, experiential passion that is itself endearing
as well as persuasive.

Phyllis Tickle
Author of *The Great Emergence*

Anyone who sets out to "live with soul, head, and hands fully engaged," as
Kyle Kramer does, is bound to lead a strenuous life. Ten years into an experiment in homesteading, he offers us a moving record of his effort to answer
the call of high ideals while meeting the demands of farming, house-building,
marriage, fatherhood, neighborliness, and a full-time job. How he found time
and energy to write these pages, and to write them so well, so honestly, so
perceptively, is a wonder. One comes away feeling it was love that set the
words flowing—love for a place, for his wife and their young children, for
good work, and for the mysterious ground from which everything rises.

Scott Russell Sanders
Author of *A Private History of Awe*

As a Franciscan, I believe the natural world has been largely lost in the Christian equation, with huge losses for the planet and our own souls. Kyle Kramer
offers you a believable, doable, and oh-so-attractive rebalancing of that equation. This book will feed your deeper hopes and perhaps a "........ ʃly" imagination that is waiting to be stirreᵈ

... ɧr, O.F.M.
· *Naked Now*

Kyle Kramer has written an i ... ve as a responsible citizen of planet Eaɽ ... ʃɪ southern Indi-
ana were the result of his fiery idealism, and at first he managed to live with
almost no carbon footprint. This is a good read and, even better, it is tonic for
the soul of anyone who wonders how to live in the twenty-first century with
a good conscience.

Terrence G. Kardong, O.S.B.
Editor of *The American Benedictine Review*

Kyle Kramer has seen and experienced that our current way of life is radically out of sorts, and that we need to stop where we are, reconsider where we got off track, and go back so we can again go forward. Wherever you are in your faith journey, you'll doubtlessly be brought into a deeper place with *A Time to Plant*.

Chris Haw
Coauthor of *Jesus for President*

A wonderfully written, thoughtfully laid out manifesto for mindful living—not so much back-to-the-land, as back-to-the-soul.

Dan Gediman
Producer of *This I Believe*

We inhabit a sacramental world wherein nature, persons, community, and their right ordering constitute a justice for which the whole creation groans. Indeed, it calls for a "vocation of location" as Kyle Kramer puts it in this fine personal narrative.

Michael Woods, S.J.
Author of *Cultivating Soil and Soul*

This narrative of an incredible undertaking in living simply confronts one of the great spiritual mysteries of contemporary life: how the desire for home can lead us into love for God, earth, and neighbor. In warm, plainspoken prose, Kramer explains how cultivating relations with land, food, and family became ways of opening himself to sustaining graces. He narrates placemaking as pilgrimage, and in doing so his meditations on spirituality and faith offer a rare, earthy wisdom.

Willis Jenkins
Author of *Ecologies of Grace*

Kyle's call to the life and work he has embraced was relentless through both his earlier years and the rich experiences the natural world showered on him. That he should find himself on ruined land with an ache to be faithful to it is a testament to the strength of a fundamental human embeddedness in earth, and to a very special longing felt by those who can move beyond the more familiar landscapes of religious fidelity. His attention, not only to the demands of new and unfamiliar details, but to the detailed way in which he shares his journey into those demands, is most helpful to the rest of us.

Miriam Therese MacGillis
Cofounder of Genesis Farm

A Time to Plant

A Time to Plant

life lessons *in* work, prayer, *and* dirt

KYLE T. KRAMER

FOREWORD BY BILL McKIBBEN

Sorin Books — Notre Dame, Indiana

Poems by Hafiz are from *I Heard God Laughing: Poems of Hope and Joy*, by Daniel Ladinsky. Copyright © 1996, 2006 by Daniel Ladinsky. Reprinted by permission of the author.

Excerpt from *That Distant Land* © 2004 by Wendell Berry. Reprinted by permission of Counterpoint.

Excerpt from *The Collected Poems of Wendell Berry, 1957–1982* © 1984 by Wendell Berry. Reprinted by permission of Counterpoint.

www.sorinbooks.com

ISBN-10 1-933495-26-X   ISBN-13 978-1-933495-26-2

Cover image © Thinkstock.

Cover and text design by Brian C. Conley.

Printed and bound in the United States of America.

Library of Congress Cataloging-in-Publication Data
Kramer, Kyle T.
  A time to plant: life lessons in work, prayer, and dirt / Kyle T. Kramer.
    p. cm.
  Includes bibliographical references.
  ISBN-13: 978-1-933495-26-2 (pbk.)
  ISBN-10: 1-933495-26-X (pbk.)
  1. Christian life--Catholic authors. 2. Home--Religious aspects--Catholic Church. 3. Farming--Religious aspects. 4. Gardening--Religious aspects--Christianity. I. Title.
  BX2350.3.K73 2010
  248.4'82--dc22

2010009721

To Cyndi, Eva, Clare, and Eli

Contents

Foreword

This is a very lovely and heartening book, and it should remind us of several things. One is that we need to be open to learning—to mentors of all kinds. It did not surprise me in the least to learn that Kyle got some of his early inspiration from the wonderful writer and teacher Scott Russell Sanders, and by extension from his guru, Wendell Berry. Nor was I surprised to learn he had a mentor, a faux uncle, who helped him find the right land and make the right plans for it. We live in a world where the easy and obvious transmission of practical knowledge, father and mother to son and daughter, has largely broken down. We need to be radically open to hearing what others have to show us.

Two is that we need to be open to where the Lord is leading us. This book offers, among other things, an interesting journey across various parts of the country, the various sects of Christianity, and the various possibilities for romantic attachment or some other path. It seems to me in reading that the author has done a more-than-average job of listening for that still small voice, and paying attention even (especially) when the advice it offers is not precisely easy to follow.

Three is that the world we are now moving into will demand of us different skills than the ones we grew up assuming we'd need. On a planet radically damaged by climate change and a host of other environmental ills, we're not going to be able to count on the remote systems that have for some decades brought us food and energy as if by magic. Instead, we will need to count on ourselves, but even more (thank heaven) on our communities. The skills of hospitality that Kyle and his wife model for us are as important as any of their talent for husbandry of the land—they remind us how we will get through the time to come, and happily.

This book and the story it tells may seem in some sense quiet, mostly confined to a small parcel of land. But it strikes me as a fine and hopeful adventure, one that should give heart to all kinds of people as they try to figure out where they're called to be. It's written with a generous spirit, less instruction and exhortation than the slightly subversive insinuation that something fine and lovely is within our grasp as well.

BILL MCKIBBEN

Introduction

What does it mean to make a home in the world? How does one live a life of faithful *belonging* to other people, to Creation, and to God? For most of my adult life, I have been driven by these questions, and my searching has taken me down an unlikely path. In 1999 I bought a rough patch of neglected ground in a rural corner of southwestern Indiana—about an hour from where I was raised and where my mother and stepfather still live—and committed myself to its healing and care. With no prior agricultural experience, by trial and error and error, I have turned it into a (mostly) working organic farm. With the help of my wife, Cyndi, many friends and neighbors, and with many smashed dreams and thumbs, I have designed and built an energy-efficient, solar- and wind-powered home on it. More importantly, I have made a commitment not only to a particular place, but to Cyndi and our children, and to the cultivation of a family life that, through all of its ups and downs, is rooted in faith as well as a meaningful connection to the natural world.

The journey to this place has at times been a bumpy one, characterized by both anxiety and hope. Taken together, these two terms capture well what I feel is the paradox of our tumultuous times. I for one am anxious because—well, who need rehearse the myriad reasons to be anxious? Will I continue to have a job and a solvent bank account to take care of those who depend on me? Will some stray nuke fall into the hands of terrorists? Will those who are rich continue to prey upon those who are poor, until desperate and deprived nations disintegrate from internal turmoil or take up arms against my country or others? Will Earth's overtaxed ecosystems collapse and make human life impossible, or merely mean and miserable—not just for distant future generations, but for my children, perhaps even for me and my contemporaries?

I am anxious about all these things and many more, and the glut of available news and information only fuels the fire of my concern. My anxiety is not just the news itself, but the realization that although I am made aware of these large-scale concerns with an immediacy that would be impossible in an earlier era, and although many of them affect me and mine, as one individual, I really cannot do a whole lot about them. I have no grand solutions to offer, nor do I foresee playing a great role on the world stage. Perhaps having so little control would be less overwhelming if I knew that someone somewhere had a sure hand on the tiller of history and could navigate the world safely toward a happy ending—or even a better, happier continuance. But, of course, such leadership is beyond any one political figure, business mogul, or sage, however talented or noble. In the end, I can't seem to muster much confidence in the large-scale plans of government or industry to build a better future. Though I know such efforts are necessary, and though I support what is best in them as my conscience allows, they are too shot through with ambiguity to bear the full weight of my trust.

On my better days, I do indeed trust that the world is in God's hands and that somehow, finally, God will bring to its fulfillment this marvelous, tragic mess that is Creation. Perhaps if my faith were not woven with threads of doubt, or if I sang hymns with more volume and conviction, I could take refuge in the idea of God as the powerful and purposeful figure who will guide us through, that "mighty fortress" who will protect us. But to be honest, I cannot begin to fathom how or when this will happen, or what cataclysms might intervene in the interim, so such a belief tends to be a cold comfort. The wholesale evils of the Holocaust, Rwanda, and Darfur have robbed me of the notion that God will step in quickly and dramatically to prevent unfathomable suffering and needless destruction, and honestly, I just can't imagine Jesus as a buff, bronzed, strong-armed warrior doing battle with the devil.

I *can* picture Jesus born quietly and unassumingly in the manger at Bethlehem. I can see Him offering food, healing, comfort—and challenge—to those in need. I can see Christ suffering and dying an ignominious death. In all of this, I suspect that God's action in our world tends to be mostly quiet, humble, easy to miss, always mysterious and often strange and ridiculous, at least at first glance.

If one takes the time to look closely, a profoundly beautiful vision of God is revealed through Jesus, but it is a vision that presents a potential problem. If Jesus reveals a subtle, enigmatic God who, rather than abolishing pain and tragedy, suffers along with us and sometimes even calls us to suffer with him, is the simple desire for a meaningful home life too pedestrian? Does it constitute a shirking of authentic Christian vocation?

Theologians more learned than I debate the ends and means of God's plans, especially in the face of terrible disaster. I am certainly searching for such answers as well, but more importantly, I am "hunting for hope," to quote a title from one of my favorite authors, Scott Russell Sanders. Although I am anxious and yearn for answers, my more immediate concern is how not to live in fear, or more to the point, in the paralysis, grumpiness, and rigidity that fear can create. I want to live with a sturdy, resilient hope rather than the much flimsier attitude of mere optimism.

I seek hope—and find it—within my Catholic Christian tradition, less perhaps in abstract theological doctrines or assurances of ultimate victory than in examples of how the life of Christian faith cultivates hope among the concrete demands of daily living. In other words, I seek (and sometimes even find) hope a bit closer to home—right at home, as a matter of fact.

Being "at home" implies being in a place or situation where you rightly belong. I believe that to be Christian is to be "on pilgrimage" in this world, but paradoxically, I also believe that learning to embrace and belong in this world is one of the essential invitations of the Christian life. After all, Christians are baptized in the name of a Trinitarian God, a God of oneness and community, one who values this world enough to have lived within it fully in Jesus, and whose own divine life is a community of Father, Son, and Holy Spirit finding a home in each other. So when I say I seek hope at home, I don't mean that I look to home simply as a spiritual retreat or refuge where I can lock myself away from the vicissitudes of an uncertain age. Rather, I see home as the place where I choose to set myself to the good but difficult challenge of authentic belonging. For me, this does not mean an attempt at self-reliance *à la* Emerson or Thoreau. Rather, it means trying to live more sweetly, more simply, and yes, more sustainably—not only for the sake of planetary and economic survival, not just out of appropriate guilt over my privilege and my oversized environmental footprint, but ultimately as a spiritual quest of conversion: in order to become my truest and best self, or as St. Irenaeus urged, to give God glory by becoming fully and truly alive.

My home happens to be an organic farm, and although farming and homesteading have been essential parts of my quest for belonging over the past ten years, I, like many of my neighbors, can afford only to farm part-time. I have been fortunate to find work that has turned into a meaningful career and vocation: directing graduate lay ministry formation programs at Saint Meinrad Archabbey, a nearby Benedictine monastery and school of theology. My journey, then, has landed me at the interesting intersection of several worlds: the pragmatic world of farming and life in a rural area; the wonderful and maddening challenges of domestic life with a wife and three young children; and the edifying, grounded community of Benedictine monks and others committed to a life of faith and service.

Out of the harmony and dissonance of these multiple worlds, I have tried to learn how to craft a saner, simpler, more just and beautiful life of belonging: a true home. I hope (and suspect) that many are yearning to do the same, for I believe such a longing is an essential part of creating a more hopeful and durable future. Whether we lead urban, suburban, or rural lives, however, most of us lack encouragement and models for creating homes that truly promote and conserve the health of our individual souls and bodies, our various communities, and our environment. The desire to find and to share hope through my small, humble efforts of making a home is what drove me to write this book.

I am no prophet, and I don't wish to throw down the gauntlet with a testy manifesto about the ideal home (as if it existed). Nor do I wish to scold those whose homes don't measure up, for I know that my own household would be the first to fail a litmus test for perfection. Instead, I would like to tell a story: my story, to some extent, but more importantly, the larger story of someone who has struggled to craft a meaningful, hope-filled life, with all of its successes and failures, joys and disappointments. My own experience is in a rural context, and so I dwell on some of the particulars of a homesteading life. But this is not a "how-to" book for simple rural living; if I were to write such a book, given all of my missteps, it would often read like a "how-not-to" book.

I have no desire to offer a recipe or a simplistic formula for cultivating hope, either. Instead, I would like to explore, through telling a bit of my story, the economy of home. By this, I mean the art of stewardship and the embrace of a "vocation of location" in which we make and maintain a particular place of belonging in the world.

Cultivating a healthy home economy includes essential, practical, never-ending domestic tasks, like preparing food (and perhaps even growing some of it), scaling mountains of dirty laundry, tackling the perpetual stack of dishes in the sink, and keeping up, more or less, with the housecleaning. For those who have some land, it includes rather extensive outdoor work, that fabulous excuse to own power equipment. It most certainly includes the dreaded and never-perfectly-balanced household budget.

More fundamentally, "home economy" means finding and creating a peaceable home in the overlapping circles of family, friends, neighbors, church, and the wider community—local and global, human and non-human. Many of us spend so much of our time at work and move so frequently from place to place that the rich concept of home has been replaced by the cheaper idea of "house," or more accurately, "McHouse": an afterthought of a place where we grab a bite to eat, watch television, escape from our jobs, make love and war with our family members, pay the bills, surf the Internet, and collapse for a few hours of sleep. Homes need to be, and can be, far more than that.

My own quixotic experience of making a home from scratch has shown me, through success and through failure, that a home can and should be a center of meaning and purpose in our lives. Home should invite us and strengthen us to the good work of belonging fully to a place and to its people. At its core, I believe that home economics is a spiritual undertaking. In his classic *Rule* governing the life of monastic communities (in some sense a kind of home-economics manual for monks), St. Benedict of Nursia emphasizes the necessary integration of work and prayer in the life of a monk. Although I am not a monk, I take Benedict's point that our material and spiritual lives are of a piece: what we do in one affects the other, for good and for ill.

Simple Living

I'm mindful that talk of "simple" or "sustainable" living can easily evoke slightly mocking images of a niche pursuit (or worse, a mere hobby, easily discarded) of educated professionals with a surplus of capital and leisure: people who donate to the Sierra Club, remember to bring cloth bags to the grocery, and purchase expensive products from environmentally conscious companies. To be clear, it is my opinion that if one doesn't hoard, waste, or become enslaved by them, having a surfeit of capital and leisure is no sin—I wish I had more of both. Abundance can, in fact, be a wonderful tool to craft a more simple life. For my part, I am grateful for people who sincerely attempt to use their abundance to live more simply. Such people help keep organic farmers in business! Hopefully this book will be of some use to them.

However, in writing this book, I hope to reach those who, like me, haven't read quite enough self-help books (or followed through on their advice), who don't quite have it all together, whose bank accounts are not flush, who aspire and hope but also stumble and sin. Because my own life includes both the pragmatic concerns of farming and family-raising among no-nonsense rural neighbors, as well as the world of Catholic ministry and spirituality, I'm interested in how simplicity and sustainability can become not just a genteel hobby, or even an earnest, well-thought-out lifestyle choice.

I'm interested in home economics as a *spiritual discipline,* as well as a realistic, practical, truly democratic trend.

At the same time, I do admit that deep down, I am a rather unapologetic idealist. It was naïve idealism that motivated me to take the leap of faith that crash-landed me in the life that I now lead—a life that, I have come to realize, is exactly the life I needed and (I believe) was called to lead. I suspect that ideals are the true drivers of both a well-lived life and any real cultural progress. It is a flat and dull life that has no idealism burning in its core.

Essential as idealism may be, especially for the Christian, it is also a recipe for pain and disappointment. Those who allow their ideals to be shaped by the Christian Gospel will eventually arrive at Calvary, the place where ideals go to die. In many ways, I see the cross as the place where our ideals and reality collide and where reality defeats them. At the cross, we discover how imperfectly our ideals have been or even can be realized—or how misguided they were in the first place.

Even if ideals lead to crucifixions, however, to my mind there is still no good reason not to hold and follow them. Perhaps the most important rite of passage of my adulthood has been the difficult negotiation between my life as I wish it to be, as I understand God would have it, and as it actually is. A significant theme woven throughout this book, then, is the challenging translation of ideals into reality, with all of the satisfactions and heartaches that translation entails.

Crucifixion is, of course, not the end of the story. To my joy, the life emerging from the tomb of my fallen ideals, while much different than the life I had once hoped for and dreamt of, is a life more full and abundant than I could have ever imagined. I like to think of it more as a gift from a faithful and loving God and less as my own construction project. So I write for fellow idealists, not to stoke false hopes or dash true ones, but to invite transformation.

Becoming an Amateur

Perfection is overrated, a wise friend once told me, and aiming for it is a recipe not only for frustration but for narcissism, since it keeps you focused on yourself and your own efforts at control rather than turning you outward in generous service to others and the planet. So even as I work to master the art of home economics, I hope to become not just a novice but a true *amateur*, a lover of what I do, even as I do it imperfectly and unprofessionally. A gentler, less anxious, more hopeful way of living rests not simply on knowledge and skill, however hard-won, but finally upon love. To be an amateur in the deepest, richest, and most life-giving sense of the word is to realize that one's home economy always unfolds within the Great Economy: a world created by God-Who-Is-Love, a world made to belong in and be at home in as both lover and beloved.

PART ONE

chapter one

Coming Home

In the oppressive, muggy air of late July, in the middle of a drought, I stumbled over the parched and cracked ground of an overgrown, weedy field in southwest Indiana. Chiggers and ticks bit; thorns and thistles scratched. I was in over my head, but not just because of the tall weeds. Though I knew next to nothing about land beyond what I'd learned from reading and dreaming, I was out there assessing this little twenty-acre patch, trying to decide if it would become my farm, my home, and my new vocation.

The small-town realtor who had come with me to attempt to sell this corner of his family home-place huffed alongside me in a sweat-soaked plaid shirt, intent upon sharing what seemed to be his family's entire century-long history of the land: what livestock had been raised on it, where the underground clay drainage tile lines lay in the field, the location of an old fencerow. Unfortunately, as I took in far more with my eyes than my ears, I could see clearly (even with comparatively untrained eyes) that the land was a mess. The woodlot had been logged the winter before, heavily and carelessly, so that many of the trees that remained were either stunted or crooked or both. Huge ruts from the logging equipment still crisscrossed the woods and fields. Tops from the felled trees had been left in the fields, where weeds and vines had all but buried them in their tangles. Saplings as thick as my wrist had grown up in the rutted fields, which had gone uncropped and unmown for several seasons. The entire place was a testament of neglect, abuse, and absentee ownership, the lack of love and care as tangible as the rough ground beneath my feet.

And yet somehow, in spite of all this, as I stood down by a dry creek bed looking northward up a gentle rise toward the road, this place, or God, or my own longing, spoke to me. I am not the type of person who tends to hear voices of divine inspiration, but in this rare moment, I heard, or perhaps felt, something clearly within me: "This place can be home to you. If all you ever do is bring this land back to health, care for it well, become a good and generous neighbor, and do all this as a prayer—that is enough." Though I couldn't recognize or articulate it at the time, that voice invited me into one of the most powerful narratives in history and literature, from the ancient Hebrews to Dorothy in the land of Oz: finding home.

The land spoke home to me, then, not because it was perfect and pristine, but because despite its ill treatment and the disarray that resulted from it, I could see that life still pulsed strong in it. I felt and hoped that I could play a role in helping some semblance of order emerge from its current chaos. I had an inkling then, and would come to believe more and more deeply over the years, that home is not the place where everything "clicks." Rather, home is a place of messy woundedness, the healing of which calls on our unique gifts and offers a unique opportunity for our own redemption.

The property that would become my home was a long, narrow rectangle, an eighth mile wide by a quarter mile deep. The northern half, which fronted a paved but little-used country road, was rough, overgrown cropland sloping down gently southward toward a creek bed lined with cedars, multiflora rose, and various scrub trees. Beyond the creek were a few acres of boggy, deep-soiled bottomland field, rank with overgrown fescue and six-foot-tall Joe Pye weeds; and south of that, a mixed-hardwood woodlot of tulip poplars, red maples, hickories, black walnuts, wild cherries, and red and white oaks. Beyond the woods on the far southern end of the property was another small field, cropped nearly to death, thick with broom sedge, maple and poplar saplings, and ragweed.

There was no county water line, gas line, or sewer hookup nearby, and even the nearest electric line was some distance away. I saw this as an advantage: it made the land less attractive to a developer and gave me a great excuse to try all the neat back-to-the-land, off-the-grid, living-lightly strategies I'd read all about in *Mother Earth News*—things like solar power, a rainwater cistern, and wood heat. The realtor and I returned to our cars, leaning on them as we picked off ticks and talked. It was a fairly decent asking price for land in rural Indiana without ready access to major utilities. I told him I'd think about it.

That evening I called my "Uncle" Ron Zimmerman, who knew of my search for land, and whose judgment I trusted better than my own. Ron was a farmer three counties west, a man who had worked himself to the bone starting a hybrid seed corn company. He had made a fair amount of money and had retired early in order to avoid a heart attack. Now he spent most of his time reading, puttering around in his immaculate garage, and roaring around the country on a shiny Harley Davidson. His son had married my sister, but the connection between us was far deeper than relation by marriage. Ron's children had not shared his lifelong love of farming and land, while my family puzzled over my newfound one. And although (or perhaps because) his farming had been large-scale and chemical-intensive, Ron could appreciate my dreams about a small, organic farm. So Ron took it upon himself to adopt me as the ersatz son on whom he could bequeath the experience he longed to share. For my part, I gratefully allowed myself to be adopted, and we forged a close bond.

Ron came out the following morning and walked the place with me. We went over it carefully, noting that it had indeed been misused but was still a fine piece of land. The heavily logged woodlot would eventually recover, Ron said. The fields still had a decent amount of topsoil and could be cleared, manured, and resown to hay or crop. There was a lovely spot on a rise near the road for a house and barn, overlooking the rest of the farm. Ron's bright blue eyes, lined both with care and experience, saw not just the mess the place was, but what it could become. In his cautious, understated way, he gave it—and me—his blessing.

In Scripture, blessings empower characters to do things that they might never dare or manage on their own power alone. God blessed Noah, and on the strength of that blessing, Noah and his family repopulated and remade the earth after the flood. God promised a blessing to Abram, which gave him the courage to leave a familiar place and people, venture out into unknown territory, and ultimately become the father of a nation. Jacob wrested his brother Esau's blessing from his father Isaac, and later, on the bank of the Jabbok, wrestled a blessing out of God, who renamed him and renewed the promise that his posterity would become the people Israel. Ron's blessing worked similarly on me. That same afternoon, I bought the property.

I had saved up a fairly significant amount of money by combining a teacher's salary and income from other part-time jobs with a fiercely spartan lifestyle. When the owner and I agreed to a price, I wrote him a check for the whole of it, signed all the paperwork, and walked out the creaking door and down the slanted steps of his old Main Street real estate office, a stunned and amazed new landowner.

It had taken me several years to become the person I needed to become to sign that check and choose a life on that piece of land. In many ways, I was the unlikeliest of persons to be drawn to either organic farming or spiritual concerns. I grew up a picky, meat-and-potatoes eater, and the few vegetables that did pass my lips did so only because of my mother's creative efforts to disguise them in to-mato popsicles and zucchini brownies (today she waxes indignant that I've become mostly vegetarian). Although I had been a Boy Scout and had done my share of camping and merit-badge-earning, I had little concern for ecology as a child; I was more interested in spending weekends tearing up the backcountry with off-road mo-torcycles and four-wheel-drive trucks and Jeeps.

In short, I was a motor-head, someone who loved fixing en-gines and all things mechanical. But by a strange twist of fate, encouraged by my artist mother, I also loved classical music and was a decent violist and tenor. I enjoyed theater and other cul-tural events, read widely, and worked hard (too hard) in school. In hindsight, what felt like a conflicted, schizophrenic existence at the time turned out to be a combination of interests that would draw me to farming and help me learn the thousand practical skills it entails.

My family and I had attended a Presbyterian church with some regularity throughout my childhood, but in those early days I had few religious feelings. I did not sense my life as part of a larger story, nor did I have a strong awareness of sin or the need for salvation—mine or anyone else's. That there was pain in the world became real to me most tangibly when, aside from the miserable growing pains associated with surviving seventh grade (which, I am convinced, rivals Dante's deepest circle of hell), I witnessed my parents' faltering marriage finally give out and end in divorce. The implosion of our family life woke me to sin, suffering, and the necessity of grace.

Perhaps as a way to cope, somewhere in my practical engineer's mind I discovered an introspective streak, one mixed with (and often fueled by) melancholy. It led me to ask questions about the deeper meaning and purpose of things. By a meandering path that led through a range of spiritual books from Norman Vincent Peale to C. S. Lewis, a dating relationship with a very evangelical Methodist, an association with para-church teen organizations like Young Life, and an Ichthus Christian music festival/revival, I said my own "yes" to the Lord. I joined and became active in the Methodist church attended by my girlfriend and her devout family and tried to follow Christ wherever he might lead.

My father worked long hours at a demanding job, and as I grew up, particularly after the divorce, he and I were not all that close. Though only much later would I discover the modern "men's movement" of Richard Rohr, Robert Bly, and others, the distance and absence I felt between us caused me to seek out, almost instinctively, a series of male mentors and father figures, all of whom shaped my thinking and nudged me in new directions. The first of these I met in college at Indiana University.

Luke Timothy Johnson, the well-known Catholic New Testament scholar and one of my professors, suffered through countless office hours of my religious questions, which had begun with my Christian conversion in high school and become more acute in college. I had admired and sought out evangelical communities during high school, impressed by their passion and by the strength of their convictions. But the rock-solid certitude that came with this particular expression of the faith seemed to leave little room for doubt, of which I had plenty—even before college. I couldn't believe that the Bible was literally inerrant, that believers of other faiths were utterly mistaken (and probably bound for hell), that concern for an imminent Apocalypse should eclipse working for justice here on Earth, or that Christianity had little useful to learn from culture, science, and other religious traditions. Luke, on the other hand, somehow had both a grounded connection to faith (he had spent ten years as a Benedictine monk) and, at the same time, the willingness to challenge it. With patience, compassion, and a razor-sharp wit, Luke nurtured my faith by welcoming my doubts—and by showing me that Christianity's expansive tradition had plenty of room for them.

If Luke invited my doubts, it was Scott Russell Sanders who helped flesh out what it might look like to put faith into action. I was able to take a small seminar with Scott my freshman year, and in that course he challenged us to discern what values animated both our culture and our economic system, and whether those values truly supported the health of communities and responsible stewardship of the natural world. The religious circles in which I had run up to that point critiqued society for its moral decadence and its failure to acknowledge Jesus but had little to say about what helped or hindered a robust civic life and the wise use of natural resources. Though Scott did not push any particular religious viewpoint, I came to see that these questions were profoundly spiritual ones, and that finding (and living) answers to them was essential to an engaged faith. I began to suspect that being Christian wasn't just about believing the right things in order to get to heaven; it also had to do with helping "thy kingdom come, on earth as it is in heaven."

Strangely, I found out only later that Scott was a well-known author and conservationist. At the time, he impressed me as much with his person as with the ideas he presented. I came to admire and respect his soft-spoken perspicacity and the gentle, humble, but firm way he challenged us sometimes-arrogant students to re-think some of our long-held assumptions. In Scott, I got to know a man who cared passionately about family, community, econo-my, and environmental health, and who made an assiduous effort to live in the world with integrity and graciousness. I wasn't quite ready to take to heart his wholesale critique of American capi-talism, individualism, and ecological insensitivity, but in who he was, what he believed, and what he practiced, Scott planted seeds of a conservation ethic that would germinate years later.

Scott in turn introduced the class to the writings of Wendell Berry, a personal friend of his and one of America's foremost cul-tural critics. We began with *The Unsettling of America: Culture and Agriculture* and its stinging critique not only of modern agri-business, but of a culture of consumption and a collective lifestyle addicted to the profligate use of cheap food, fossil fuels, and raw materials. I soon also discovered Wendell's novels and poetry, of which I couldn't read enough. I found myself captivated by his keen and prophetically blunt critique of modern American culture, his simple, self-sufficient rural lifestyle on a farm in his native northern Kentucky, and his vision of an economy and culture more in harmony with the natural world. An instant fan, I wrote him a letter, inviting him to give a series of lectures at Indiana Universi-ty. Not long after, I realized that I had foolishly asked him, a farm-er, to come for a week during planting season! He refused politely, but this exchange began an occasional correspondence that has continued through the present. Through his published work, our letters, and a visit or two, Wendell has had a profound influence on my thinking and my life choices, even as he rightly encouraged me to discover my own path rather than simply emulate his. Like Scott, Wendell showed me that a truly healthy culture and econo-my depended on a healthy relationship with the Great Economy:

the divinely designed and governed world of nature. Wendell also insisted that meaningful change almost always begins and is sustained at the local level, and that individual life choices should reflect not just one's personal ethical commitments, but one's vision of the ideal society.

I spent my junior year of college studying at the University of Hamburg, Germany, and did a good deal of traveling throughout eastern and western Europe. While there, I got to know public transportation, recycling, and other habits of a society that, while quite advanced, seemed far more intentional (and gentle) than ours. I still remember marveling at how a work crew, fixing a waterline near my apartment, carefully dug up concrete sidewalk pavers—without damaging them—and then proceeded to repair the line. After the repairs were completed, they painstakingly returned the sidewalk to its place. I noted with sadness how in America, workers would likely have simply jack-hammered the sidewalk, tossed it into a dumpster, and poured new concrete.

It was also in Germany, specifically while traveling in "godless" East Germany, of all places, that I began to make connections between the life of faith and tangible acts of justice. As part of a research project on the role of the Church in the fall of communism, I met and interviewed several East German Christians whose living, breathing, oftentimes defiant faith had led them to take great personal risks and suffer great hardship as they worked for social change. Their material lives were simple and humble by force of circumstance and yet had a richness and authenticity I envied.

My time abroad also introduced me to a sense of the sacred, mainly through church architecture. I was awed by the majestic cathedrals and basilicas in Cologne, Rome, and elsewhere. These structures were a testament to a faith that had moved mountains of stone and fashioned earthbound materials into edifices that reached to the heavens. Even though the decline of Christianity in Europe made them more like museums than vibrant centers of worship, they still had the power to inspire. When I returned to America, the Christianity I came back to seemed fairly pedestrian, more inclined toward personal piety than beauty and transcendence. My discontent grew, and as part of the coursework for my religious studies major, I explored other religious traditions. Ironically, it was a course on Hinduism that ultimately clarified an essential element of my Christian vocation.

I was drawn to study Hindu practice because it seemed so embodied, so *real*, so enmeshed in the world of the body and the senses. When worshippers offer devotion to their gods, Hindu temples are filled with festive colors, the sounds of chanting and song, the smells of incense and food offerings, and the bodily movements of dance or various ascetic exercises. I related this to the professor in a conversation, and he named something essential that I was struggling to discover; what I had missed in the Christianity I had known, and what I was so drawn to in Hinduism, was a sense of sacramentality: a way of believing and practicing that was intimately connected with the world, that valued and embraced the world even as it sought spiritual enlightenment. This professor, himself a Hindu married to a Catholic, told me that I didn't need to abandon my tradition; he recommended that I look to the sacramental and liturgical expressions of Christianity, namely the Orthodox, Anglican, and Catholic traditions, to find the sort of incarnated faith for which I'd been longing.

At the invitation of a friend, I began attending Catholic Masses for the first time. I felt bewildered and confused by much of the ceremony and put off by a long prejudice against what I thought of as the stubborn backwardness of Catholic doctrine. But in the liturgy itself I found something real and tangible, something I knew I'd been missing up to then. I was drawn to this incarnated

Christian faith, but I didn't seriously consider *becoming* Catholic. Who in their right mind would join a church that insisted on a celibate, male clergy, the authority of the pope and magisterium, and other such anachronisms? At the time, the Episcopal Church seemed like a reasonable compromise: all the richness of tradition, a smells-and-bells liturgy, and a sacramental imagination, with none of the inconveniences of Catholicism.

Undergraduate degrees in religious studies and German aren't exactly a first-class ticket to a high-paying career, or any career for that matter. I knew I wanted to pursue both theological and cultural questions more deeply after graduation, and I seriously considered the idea of an academic career and ordination as an Episcopal priest. After graduating from Indiana University, I enrolled in the Candler School of Theology at Emory University in Atlanta, Georgia.

My graduate school years in Atlanta were wonderfully rich and challenging, and my education took place both in and beyond the classroom. In class, I delved into biblical studies, ethics, history, and other disciplines of theology. As part of my degree, I did supervised ministry as a chaplain in a drug rehabilitation center, which was my first real introduction to the rough world of addiction. I got to know Duane, a devout Muslim convert whose piety was the motivation for his desperate attempt to get clean. I encountered Chester, a belligerent addict who bounced in and out of treatment and who was trying to get off drugs because his habit interfered with his pimping. I came face to face with my own fears, prejudices, and snobbery.

I also realized that but for a few different choices or circumstances, I could have been one of those to whom I was trying to minister. My interaction with people in recovery led me to suspect that, black or white, rich or poor, addicted or clean, we are all just a few short steps from either salvation or disaster. Sadly, I saw that for many in recovery, traditional religion was actually an obstacle to healing; for many, it was a guilt-stick with which they beat themselves or a pious fantasy behind which they hid their real selves. For a few, however, religion was a true path to humility: a lens through which they saw clearly their own brokenness, but also their belovedness and the possibility of their redemption.

Outside school, I decided to begin taking sustainable living seriously, sometimes with comic results. I experimented with an electricity-free "simple living" boot camp, when, for a few months, I forsook lights, my range, air-conditioning, and the refrigerator. I tried my best not to advertise what I was doing, but when I startled evening visitors by coming to the door with a kerosene lantern, I soon earned a reputation for "uniqueness" among my friends and neighbors.

I spent a lot of time connecting with the natural world, both wild and cultivated. I often backpacked in the north Georgia mountains along the Appalachian Trail and other routes. Ironically, while I loved the time in the wilderness, my first truly deep connection with nature took place right outside my back door in the middle of downtown Atlanta. The school-owned apartment complex where I lived backed up on the steep, wooded, and largely undisturbed valley of Peachtree Creek. I spent countless hours roaming among the huge old oaks and pignut hickories, learning to identify trees and edible wild plants, writing poetry by the bank of the creek, and paying attention night and day to how the stars and sun wheeled across the sky through each season.

One late night in winter, I leaned against an old hickory and looked up its tall, straight, thick trunk, through its leafless branches, to the starry sky above. A gust of wind caught the branches, and I felt a subtle movement through the entire tree. In that moment I felt deeply how *alive* the tree was. While I spent my time up the hill in my apartment studying dead theologians or worrying about paper deadlines and grades, the tree pulsed with its own life, accumulating its own unique sort of experience, memory, and after a fashion, wisdom. No wonder, I thought, that the environmentalists hug trees.

Wanting to put into practice some of my growing environmental interests, I sought permission to dig up a patch of grass in the apartment complex, and with the help of another Candler student—a quiet, sweet, middle-aged Quaker woman named Sharon—I made my first garden. We established it as a community organic garden for the residents of the apartment complex, and over my years of gardening in Atlanta, I not only learned the arts of cultivation, but I saw how the simple, essential work of growing food would draw neighbors together and give them, quite literally, "common ground" for relating to each other and to the earth. Gardening became a refuge from the intensity of my studies, placing them in a broader perspective and grounding me amid the crises of faith, character, and vocation that are part and parcel of any theological education. Against the background noise of rumbling traffic, honking horns, and the general bustle of city life, the gardens I tended provided an oasis of calm and timelessness.

Gardening also precipitated a crisis, however. As time went on and I progressed in graduate school, I could not help but notice that the fruits of my labors in the garden brought me far more satisfaction than did the fruits of my labors in the library and the classroom. I felt a tension similar to what I had experienced in high school when I was a musician, earnest overachieving student, and gear-head: on the one hand, exploring the magnificent intellectual architecture of the Christian theological tradition; on the other, tending gardens, reading about agriculture, attending sustainable farming conferences, getting to know organic farmers in the area, and working on a variety of organic farms during the summers. Paradoxically, it seemed that parts of me were soaring up into the heavens, even as other parts were rooting themselves deeply in the earth. I felt torn between the two.

Someone might wonder why I did not simply work harder to strike a balance between garden and library. I suppose I could have; such a balance is certainly possible. Looking back, however, I realize the tension I felt had less to do with some fundamental incompatibility between these realms than with two competing ways of approaching life. I had always done well in the academic realm, but as often as not, my success came from a competitive, ego-driven desire for achievement and recognition. Gardening, however, was a more humble practice of nurture, community, true learning for the sake of doing, and the lack of absolute control. In this area, I was a novice. I suspect that gardening could have eventually taught me a healthier way to function in the academic realm and in life generally. But at the time, I was not ready for that lesson, so I had no idea how to reconcile school and dirt.

Until I discovered gardening, my plans were fairly set: ordination, doctoral work in theology, and a distinguished academic career alongside serving as an Episcopal priest—and of course, marrying the perfect woman and raising the perfect family. But the tension between the practical and the ethereal, which had always been present in me but came to a head in seminary, brought about a tectonic shifting of my plans and dreams, and I found myself pitched into unknown vocational territory.

In retrospect, this was precisely what I needed, for I have come to believe that both humility and vocational clarity can come only after a period of disorientation and doubt, when many of our certainties have been swept away. At the time, however, the tensions and collisions between my academic work and my agricultural

interests did not feel like lessons in humility and true vocation—
they felt a lot like crisis. Academic achievement had always come
easy and had been central to my identity, but as I thought more
about agriculture, I often found myself with next to no motivation
to do my schoolwork. While I slogged on through and performed
well enough (due mostly to perfectionist discipline), I slowly became both horrified and humiliated to discover how my heart
could disengage from something that I had always thought would
be a cornerstone of my vocational path.

I wrote a letter to Wendell Berry, wondering whether I should
give up my pursuit of a degree in favor of pursuing a farming
life. He was quick to write back, firmly but kindly, that farming was a very hard living and that I would do well to have my
degree to fall back on. I pressed on with the Master of Divinity,
but even as I did so, the dream of a farming life began to take
more tangible shape: a life of simplified needs and wants; a gentle, rich, generous life lived close to the land, close to the heart,
close to the heartbeat of all that I considered real and important.
Such a life, it seemed to me, would be the culmination of theological training, personal growth, and service to others and the
planet. As the vision of this life became clearer to me, it began
to eclipse the vision that had brought me to Atlanta in the first
place. Eventually, I came to the conclusion that my obedience to
the calling of this sort of lifestyle would have to come before my
obedience to a bishop and a priestly vocation. If I couldn't look
a bishop in the eye and say with utter conviction that I would go
wherever I was sent and fulfill any assignment I was given, then
I wasn't ready to consider ordination. For similar reasons, I realized that I also wasn't ready for doctoral study, locked up in a
library, with no guarantee of a job when I finished. It would keep
me away that much longer from the sort of life I envisioned. This

discernment took place over several months, but as it unfolded, I sensed the quiet collapse of all my well-laid plans.

What made this crisis in vocation tolerable were relationships, especially those I found at Holy Comforter Church, an Episcopal mission parish in a run-down part of southeast Atlanta. When I arrived in the city, I first attended a large, wealthy downtown Episcopal Church with a very charismatic pastor and many active ministries. I enjoyed being part of that community. It was there that I went through catechetical instruction and officially joined the Episcopal Church. Eventually, however, I became less and less comfortable nosing my Ford past the security guard in the parking lot in order to park it between a spotless BMW and a gleaming Lexus. I soon sought out a parish closer to Emory, whose vicar I admired and whose smaller, more neighborly feel meshed better with my sensibilities. I worshipped there for a while, but when a seminary friend invited me to join him one Sunday at the Church of the Holy Comforter, I was hooked from the first. I knew, soul-deep, that this was the place where I belonged.

Holy Comforter is an inner-city Atlanta parish with a mission to serve poor, mentally and physically disabled men and women who live nearby in group homes. In many ways it embodies the spirit of Jean Vanier's L'Arche communities, which were such an inspiration to the writer Henri Nouwen. Like L'Arche, Holy Comforter is a place where, amid much brokenness, community grows out of mutual vulnerability, transparency, and acceptance. This was a jolt to my overachiever's mentality, but being part of Holy Comforter turned out to be an essential grace at a time when I needed it most.

My first reflex was to help out in whatever ways I could: driving battered old vans to bring parishioners to church, working in the church's organic gardens, singing and playing guitar at Masses, and serving at our regular community meals and parish activities. After a while, however, I began to realize that whatever service I offered was far less than the great gift the men and women of that parish gave me: a sense of belonging that didn't require me to have it all together, and a place where I could admit that my plans had faltered and that I was unsure of the road ahead. I got to know a God who promised to be with me and love me whether or not I was successful or well-published. Surrounded by people who lived so much out of their hearts, I began to realize that even if my dreams were small and my efforts toward them stumbling, their value would depend on the quality of heart with which I pursued them.

Holy Comforter's pastor at the time, Fr. Mark Baker, was a former operatic baritone and a gentle, easy-going, fun-loving man in his forties. Mark loved serving the parish, but his other passion was woodworking. He and I connected well, and he served as a great mentor and spiritual advisor for the years I was involved with the parish. Unlike most people I knew from graduate school, Mark understood the strong need I had to connect the spiritual, the intellectual, and the *manual*: to live with soul, head, and *hands* fully engaged. This integration was an essential gift for the sort of ministry he did at Holy Comforter. Mark outfitted the church with pottery and sculpting equipment as well as woodworking tools, and he created programs for the parishioners that allowed them to engage in all sorts of arts and crafts, helping them to create birdhouses, coat racks, mugs, candlesticks, and various clay sculptures that were sold in local art shows and festivals. He and I talked regularly, but we also worked together, both in his home shop and at the church.

Mark and Holy Comforter gave me a profound gift: permission to take risk and permission to fail. As I befriended Holy Comforter's mentally and physically disabled parishioners, I got to know the profound wisdom, goodness, and beauty of people (and, yes, their meanness, selfishness, and self-destructiveness, too) who, by any typical standard, were utter failures. Encountering these people, I came to realize that such external standards did not accurately measure—let alone bestow—the worth, value, or dignity of a human being. If such folk didn't need to live up to certain standards in order to be loved and valued by God, then perhaps neither did I.

As my dreams for ordination and an academic career were fading and new dreams to replace them were still inchoate and unformed, I felt a tremendous sense of loss, grief, failure, and shame that I wasn't living up to the expectations my life's trajectory had set up for me—the expectations of others, certainly, but even more mercilessly, my own standards. Somehow, the community of Holy Comforter held me and loved me, even as I saw myself as a failure, and in that embrace, failure felt friendlier and less threatening. And if failure wasn't so bad, if I could still feel loved and accepted in the midst of it, then risking failure wasn't as dangerous as I'd always believed. As my new dreams of a simpler life on a small farm began to take shape, Mark encouraged me, reminding me that sooner rather than later was the best time to make an attempt at such a life, and that the worst that might happen is that I would discover I didn't care for it or couldn't handle it, and so then I could move on to whatever dream might come to take its place.

After graduating from Emory, I stayed on in Atlanta. I lived, worshipped, and came to belong more deeply at Holy Comforter. I gave what I could and learned what I could. I pared down my life to its barest essentials, and to support myself and save for the farm I was dreaming about, I took a position teaching English and German at Ben Franklin Academy, a very expensive private high school whose students were children of the elite who had not thrived in other public and private schools due to learning disabilities, behavioral problems, and trouble with drugs, alcohol, or the law. Having landed the job through friends I knew at Holy Comforter who also taught at the school, I was able to work with not only some amazing kids, but some remarkably patient, loving, and kind-hearted fellow teachers.

From the students, who came mainly from wealthy Atlanta families, I discovered how a life of privilege can have an ugly underbelly: lack of discipline and focus, impatience, overindulgence, and addiction. I saw kids struggle and prevail over all of these with the support of the school. I also saw kids struggle and *not* prevail, as when Jesse, a student I cared about deeply, could no longer take the pressures of school, friends, parents, and a drug addiction. He finally escaped these pressures by shoving a handgun into his mouth.

At his funeral, the well-intentioned but unfortunate eulogy whitewashed Jesse. It made him into a well-liked, popular, happy, industrious young man—the young man, I suspect, his grieving family wanted and needed to remember, though he was none of these things. It would have been far more difficult but far more honest to acknowledge the dark mystery of his suffering and addiction, and to proclaim that even in this, he was held by a God who suffered with him and wanted only to love him back to health. I know the family meant well, but the funeral was the polar opposite of my experience at Holy Comforter, where the love of Christ was shown in a love that embraced the gritty reality of poverty, addiction, and disability.

At the school, amid all of the tears and tortured conversations afterward, both teachers and students realized how precious and fragile our enterprise really was. We were trying to create a safe haven for these kids and were doing so with some success. And yet so much could fall apart so quickly.

Any life is fragile, of course, but the experience at Ben Franklin, especially in contrast to the experience of Holy Comforter, showed me that I wanted a life built on values far more solid than wealth, achievement, appearances, and social status. Values like these seemed rickety at best, and not only for those who were especially troubled, as Jesse was. Any of them could give way at a moment's notice, for reasons totally beyond one's control. Even if a person could manage to avoid their collapse, the life based on them would be a lie. We're *all* broken. None of us is the master of our fate. We belong to a whole much larger and more wonderful than ourselves, and we all need love and grace as the cornerstones of our belonging.

I wanted a life that acknowledged these truths; one that would rest on durable values that really mattered, both to me and to the good of the world. Though I had been ambitious for much of my life, I began to see that ambition was not a deep truth of who I was and not what God wanted for me. My calling was to a life whose exterior might seem small and insignificant but that cultivated an interior spaciousness and centeredness. I wanted a life that was grounded in acts of justice and awareness of divine mercy, a life connected intimately to other people and to the rest of Creation.

Of course there is no one mold for such a life. I suspect there are as many lives that incarnate these values as there are people who imagine them. For my part, I felt drawn to rural living. Though I certainly had my share of naïveté, I did not envision this as an escape from the urban rat race to some pristine pastoral paradise. I knew then and see even more clearly now that the landscapes and people of both city and country are wounded, often in surprisingly similar ways. I simply saw the rural environment as the one that suited me best, the place where I wanted to cast my lot and make my stand.

The country seemed to be the place, and farming the life, in which the various tensions in me—the mechanic and the poet, the spiritual seeker and the lover of earth, the pragmatist and the ideal-ist, the task-oriented and the contemplative—had the best chance of reconciling. And if through this life God could help me be-come more whole, then it would be through this life that I might do whatever healing and hopeful work I could for others and the Creation. A simple vision began to take shape with more and more clarity: living on a small farm; growing healthy food and steward-ing the land well; building an energy-efficient, "green" home; and investing myself in the needs and gifts of the local community. I felt a deep conviction that this vision was not only what I imag-ined for my life, but what God was imagining for it as well: a true vocation to which I was called to be faithful.

It was, by necessity, a long-term vision. Being averse to debt and wanting to ensure that I could live on little by avoiding a hefty mortgage payment, I made the crazy decision that I would save up enough cash to buy land and build a little cabin on it. I bided my time, living on practically nothing, saving money fiercely, and dreaming of land and farms. About a year into this rhythm, I made a retreat to a Trappist monastery in Conyers, Georgia, and met with a spiritual director. I stared at his sandaled feet as I described my im-patience with my current urban existence and my desire to pursue a simple, agrarian life. To be honest, I didn't find the director all that helpful, or even all that sane, but at one point he looked at me (at least I think he did, since his eyes focused somewhat independently of each other) and asked if I thought the Holy Spirit might be calling me to embrace that dreamed-of life. "Yes, I do," I replied, going on about my plans and my responsible, several-year timetable. "No," he interrupted. "I think the Spirit is calling for you to go, *now*."

When that half-crazy old monk spoke those few simple words, it was as if a switch had been thrown in me. I knew I wasn't ready (would I ever be?) and I didn't have enough money saved up, but somehow his words rang true. I knew I had to go. Already I could feel all of the moorings to my current life begin to snap, one by one. Dazed, I returned to Atlanta and met with Fr. Mark. He confirmed that now was the time. "You're young, you're strong, you're motivated, you're single, and you have some money saved up," he assured me. "You're *ready*, even if you don't think you are. And what do you have to lose? Why not try it now? If all else fails and you end up miserable, at least you know it isn't the life for you, and you're still young enough to try something else." He was right, of course, and it was the second kick in the tail I needed to get moving.

The next several weeks were a blur. I met with Ben Franklin's headmaster, explained my situation, and told him that I likely wouldn't be returning to teach the following year. The headmaster generously encouraged me to look for land, and we agreed on a date by which I would let him know if I would continue to teach. I then spent much of the summer making trips to Indiana, pursuing any real estate leads I could find. I scoured the ads. I stopped by the roadsides to talk to farmers in their fields. I went to 4-H fairs, equipment dealers, and anyone I could find to see if they knew of a small piece of land that might be for sale at agricultural prices. I looked longingly at a patch of ground so steep that it would roll a tractor, convincing myself that I could terrace it and farm it nonetheless; only the seller's sheepish admission that a planned interstate would soon bisect the land dissuaded me from the purchase. I looked at a landlocked 40-acre parcel whose only access was a narrow easement past a grubby, moldy, cinder-block hovel with a yard littered with trash, derelict cars, and broken children's toys. I looked and looked and didn't find.

Finally, after weeks of intense but fruitless searching, I made a decision. I had been looking for land all over Indiana and Kentucky, figuring that this would increase my chances of finding something I could afford. But then another bolt of lightning struck in my consciousness. One of the key drivers in this process was my desire to come "home," back to the place of my roots, back to the region where my family still lived. I came to realize that my search lacked focus, and I decided that if I was going to move back home, I should *really* move back home. I took out a map of Indiana, set a compass to a distance of thirty miles as the crow flies, put the center point on my mother and step-father's home, and drew a circle around that point. One of my hopes was to nurture a closer relationship with my parents, and I came to realize that even living two hours away meant we would likely go months between visits. If I were ever to get married and have children, I would want them to grow up having familiarity with their grandparents. So I committed to restricting my search to within that circle. I remember praying boldly that night, almost daring God to defy my commitment. I would commit to seeking and buying land within the thirty-mile radius; God would have to provide the land. That's all there was to it.

My wandering in the wilderness did not last the forty years that the Israelites' did, but it seemed to stretch on interminably. Having made the geographical commitment to my parents, I felt like I'd nailed one foot to the floor and was madly circling around it. The summer was winding down, and I was approaching the absolute deadline by which I would need to recommit to another year's teaching. Frustrated and despairing, even grumbling a bit like the Israelites, I walked one August morning into a realtor's office on Main Street in the Ohio River town of Rockport,

Indiana. I met with a nice woman who showed me a variety of listings, none of which I wanted or could afford. Then another re-altor, who shared the office and had overheard our conversation, let me know that although he hadn't listed it yet, he was trying to sell off part of his home-place, following his father's recent death. I agreed to follow him out to the property, which was at the outer limits of my thirty-mile search radius. The following day, I owned the land, free and clear. My mom and stepdad agreed to let me live with them as I built some sort of shelter and set the farm to rights. With these plans made, I returned to Atlanta. I gave notice at Ben Franklin, the community of Holy Comforter sent me off with a celebration, and I tied up the loose ends of my life there.

Saying goodbye to the city was not difficult, for I had long felt claustrophobic, surrounded by a concrete moat of interstate beltway. Saying goodbye to my friends and fellow parishioners at Holy Comforter, however, felt like a disembowelment. Every leave-taking reminded me of the good things I was leaving be-hind, exchanging them for a future that was completely unknown. I had no job lined up, no idea how to start a farm or build a house, no real plan—what was I thinking?

Once again it was a blessing from the parishioners at Holy Comforter that finally helped me let go of all that I held dear in Atlanta. At the ceremony, I wept as my poor, physically and men-tally handicapped friends laid their hands on me and sent me into my new life. When I asked Fr. Mark how I could keep Holy Com-forter in my heart, he told me that the best way to carry this com-munity with me would be to give myself fully to this new vocation and to pursue it as faithfully as I could. Somehow, sent off with the love of my friends, I knew I would be able to manage; I knew, in a place far deeper than my intellect, that the God who called me to this new life would not leave me desolate. Not too many days later,

I packed a yellow rental truck with my belongings, hitched up my car to it, and headed north, back home into the great unknown.

chapter two

Settling In

Iarrived back in Indiana in early September 1999. Pulling my rental truck into the entrance drive of the gated golf-course community where my parents had moved after I left for college, I was overcome by a sickening feeling that I had no business buying a farm. Up to this point, I had convinced myself that I possessed what was required to thrive in a simple, rural lifestyle: there was my Boy Scout experience, of course, and I had grown up loving the outdoors and working with my hands. But in the final analysis, although I'd spent some summers visiting and working on various organic farms, my parents' housing development was more representative of my life experience. I came from small-town suburbia. My parents were educated professionals who had been raised by a machinist, a secretary, a shoe salesman, and a seamstress. I had no farming in my blood, much less in my immediate experience. Though I had played endlessly outside as a child, all in all I had been a spectator of the landscape around me rather than an active steward.

If a more sustainable society requires repopulating and revitalizing our rural areas, as I now believe to be the case, inevitably such a movement will mean that some ignorant, inexperienced folk like myself will have to charge headlong into alien territory and acquire, largely from scratch, skills and knowledge they never fathomed. I'd fallen in love with farming mostly in the abstract, as a romantic notion and moral ideal. Organic farming sounded so right, so wholesome and satisfying, so unequivocally good! And building your own house and homestead, to boot—how much more primal can you get than food, water, and shelter? What would be closer to an agrarian ideal and to the best of the American pioneer spirit?

What faced me as I parked the truck, however, was terrifyingly concrete, and I didn't miss the irony of having made, at age twenty-six, what I thought was a bold, courageous, principled leap of faith into a new life, and landing in a bedroom of my parents' basement. I lived with them for several months and, while there, experienced a cauldron of emotions. I was grateful for their hospitality and unfailing encouragement and support, yet restless to be out on my own on my land. I was excited by the projects that lay before me, but overwhelmed as I realized their scope and complexity. Long before I deserved the title, I was proud to tell people I was an organic farmer. The pride I experienced was almost— but not quite—strong enough to overcome the embarrassment that my situation was closer to what is more commonly known as unemployment.

If the process of purchasing farm equipment was any indicator of my future success, I should have quit within the first few weeks, as I made one misjudgment after the next. I found a late-seventies-era Ford four-wheel-drive pickup listed in the classifieds, and my stepdad drove me out to take a look at it. A beat-up, worn-out old firewood hauler, it was rusty, dented, and rough. The owner was pretty rough too, and he would not even allow me to test drive the truck, making some excuse that his insurance wouldn't cover me. So he took me for a spin in it. The big V8 engine roared as we creaked and bounced down the road, and the loose front end wandered about like a drunken sailor. When we returned to his place, I heard a hissing sound, and opened the hood to discover the radiator was squirting coolant from a pinhole leak. The truck was a worthless junk pile, all around. But impulsiveness ruled the day, so I haggled him down $150 off the asking price, wrote a check, and drove it home.

I hadn't even made it home when I was overcome by a tidal wave of buyer's remorse—or in this case, plain old common sense. This purchase was not an auspicious beginning to my farming career, but by the time I got the truck home, I determined that I would not throw good money after bad. So I spent a day fixing the truck's glaring mechanical problems, slapping body filler into rust holes, sanding and priming, and trying to make the truck look even passably better than when I'd bought it. I called the newspaper and placed an ad for the truck. When it came out the following day, I cringed to find my ad and the previous owner's ad running right next to each other.

Buddhism makes the claim that life is impermanent and that all things are transient. In this particular instance, I was glad to learn that the laws pertaining to the buying and selling of old trucks seemed to uphold that claim. Within a few days I was fortunate to find a new buyer for the truck, a mechanic more willing and able than I to tackle its various problems. I walked away having lost only $100, a lot of pride, and a few days' worth of worry and work. It was a cheap lesson learned, although I feared what expensive lessons might lie ahead.

Looking back after ten years of similar mistakes, I'm grateful to have avoided any catastrophic blunders. I didn't realize then, though I see clearly now, how easily an endeavor such as mine could be sabotaged by impatience, impulsiveness, and an unwillingness to admit fallibility or mistakes—and how difficult it is to outgrow such traits. They may end up dogging our every step.

The rest of my shopping proceeded much more cautiously. I bought a freshly painted 1953 Ford Golden Jubilee tractor and kicked my stepdad's car out of the garage so I could park it inside until I could get it out to the farm. I found a newer, more sensible and sedate, more expensive but reliable Ford pickup, which I christened "Big Blue." I picked up a brand-new sixteen-foot trailer, which I used to transport the tractor and a variety of implements out to the farm.

Having a comfortable place to live and no clear idea what sort of shelter I should build on the farm, I spent most of that first fall trying to get the fields in order. I spent many days with a chainsaw, dismembering the fallen treetops that littered the field, stacking the cut logs at the field edges for eventual use as firewood. My little Ford tractor struggled to power a brush mower through rutted fields overgrown with six-foot-tall weeds. It didn't take me long to realize that a fresh coat of paint does not a rebuilt tractor make, and I cursed myself for having bought another piece of junk, albeit one with a better paint job. The tractor ran hot and had a mysterious problem of running perfectly for a few minutes and then stalling out and not restarting for half an hour.

Late one afternoon the tractor died out hundreds of yards away from my truck and tools. I lugged the toolbox down to it, trying to wrench it back to life. In a rather spectacular temper tantrum, I became so angry and frustrated that I started flinging my tools into the nearby woods, along with a barrage of curse words that would take the bark off a tree. Ashamed of both my incompetence and my immature emotional reaction, I felt completely and utterly defeated. When I purchased the farm, I had made in my mind a covenant to care for it. Now I felt I was unworthy of ownership and incapable of the good work the land required of me. I felt that all of my romantic notions of farming were being ground to pieces under the heel of what real farm work actually entailed. I felt, in other words, that I would never belong here.

Tears of discouragement were welling up when I saw some movement at the corner of the field and turned to see a figure walking toward me across the brush. A soft-spoken, shy man in his forties, he introduced himself as John Schaeffer. He'd heard that someone had bought part of the Brinkman place, and when he was driving by and saw my truck, he walked down through the fields to find me and say hello.

After our introductions, he turned to the tractor. "That thing giving you some trouble?" he asked in a gentle, quiet voice. Ruefully realizing that he'd likely heard my tirade of curses (that was probably how he located me), I described the symptoms with as much calm as I could muster. John almost immediately diagnosed the problem—a partially clogged fuel valve. Using a piece of baling wire (of course!), within a few minutes he had the little four-cylinder purring sweetly. I thanked him profusely, but he waved it off. "Don't think about it," he replied. "Welcome to the neighborhood."

In rural areas with low population density, the word "neighborhood" takes on a new definition. I can count on one hand, with a few fingers left over, the number of houses within a half-mile radius of my property. Rather than being a small, neat, and tidy subdivision with cookie-cutter houses, cul-de-sacs, and a vicarious name like Windemere Farms, my neighborhood encompasses many square miles of real farms. A ragtag collection of nice new brick homes, weathered old farm houses, mobile homes, and double-wides are small pinpoints on a landscape otherwise given to rolling corn and soybean fields, woodlots, hayfields, pastures, grain silos, and farm outbuildings. But as John had showed me, the *idea* of neighborliness and courtesy still ran strong here, even embracing an outsider like I was.

Not a man of many words, John explained how to find his farm a few miles south, told me to stop by some time or call if I needed something, and then trudged back up to the top of the hill and eased his rusty old Dodge pickup truck back onto the road. As he left, I scavenged the woods for my end wrenches and pliers, and I felt a glimmer of hope about the life I'd embarked upon. One person, at least, had reached out a hand and kept me from drowning in my own misery and incompetence. John had been an angel sent to save my hide, and from that very first meeting, he has been a wonderful neighbor.

The autumn work continued in earnest, and frustration gave way to occasional glimpses of what the land could become if given the love and attention it needed. The fields, as they were cleared of toppled trees, saplings, and head-high weeds, actually began to look something like fields again, rather than fledgling forests. I spent a day in early November doing chainsaw work. Throughout the day I'd felt a strange ambiguity about my task, as my saw disturbed the silence with its raucous roar and spewed clouds of dirty exhaust from its two-cycle engine. Nature had quieter, more efficient, ultimately more beautiful ways of taking care of such things. But as I was learning, even an "organic" farm isn't simply nature left to its own devices. In southern Indiana, as my five-years-fallow fields bore witness, nature left alone turns cleared farm fields back into mixed-hardwood forest in fairly short order. It hit home with some discomfort that a farm—or any place of human habitation, for that matter—is nature disturbed, nature harnessed, nature tamed to some degree, nature with a human will imposed on it. The question is not whether or not we will tamper with nature, for we have and we will; the question is how gently, wisely, humbly, and cleverly we do the tampering—and why.

I did not feel gentle, wise, humble, or clever as I shut down the chainsaw for the evening; I felt tired. I packed up my equipment as the light faded, drove my pickup to the top of the highest rise on the farm, and propped myself up in the bed of the truck to watch the sun set. Even though the chill night air seeped through my clothes, I stayed long enough to watch the sun sink below the western tree line, and I stayed longer still until all traces of the day were gone. The night sky became a pitch-black canvas, and a multitude of stars appeared as the faint stripe of the Milky Way stretched north and south. After a day of manhandling a noisy machine, the silence—almost complete and total—felt soft, sweet, and full of forgiveness. I felt that the Creation, in its patience and wisdom, was not only tolerant of my clumsy efforts, but that both Creation and Creator accepted them. That evening, I felt like I *could* truly belong in this place and in this world. I felt blessed and at home. The world, at least in that moment, seemed above all a place of mercy and benevolence.

Nature may have been kind, but she was also cold—by late November, frost lightened the ground almost every evening. With the coming of winter and the land looking much improved, I turned my thoughts toward shelter. As welcoming and hospitable as my mom and stepdad had been, the comfort of a room in your parents' basement—even when you are in a tight spot—lasts only so long. I wanted my own place, on my own land. And I now had a growing fleet of machines and equipment that needed to be under a roof.

I knew I wasn't ready to build both a house and a barn. I lacked the money and had no chance of getting a mortgage without a paying job. So for the time being, I simply needed something small, simple, and affordable. After much head-scratching, I decided to follow in the footsteps of many in this area: I would build a big, metal-sided "pole barn" in which I could keep vehicles and farm equipment. I would then finish out a very small part of it as an apartment.

I reasoned that if I built a more permanent home later, the apartment could become a studio, a workshop, or even an abode for my parents as they aged. Or, if I stayed single, I could probably live out my days in the apartment and never get around to erecting anything more substantial. In addition, building a pole barn with an apartment would give me a chance to hone my construction skills on a more forgiving job than that of building a full-sized house. So I sketched out a design for a large barn with a smallish one-bedroom apartment tucked into a back corner. True to my back-to-the-land ambitions, I planned to install solar panels on the barn roof for my electricity, a cistern that would catch rainwater off the roof for my water supply, and a waterless composting toilet: an independent homestead with no utility bills save for some propane needed to run a gas stove and water heater.

Through a few phone calls, I found someone nearby to come out with a backhoe and level off the building site and cut a driveway out of the roadbank. After he finished up his work, he and I got to chatting. Dressed in beat-up old Carhartt coveralls and eyeing my decidedly yuppie-looking Gore-tex hiking jacket, he asked, "So, you from around here?"

"Yeah," I answered enthusiastically, desperately wanting to seem like I fit in. "I'm from Darmstadt," I said, naming the small 1,200-person hamlet that was, in truth, a bedroom community to the much larger city of Evansville, Indiana.

Seeing through this subterfuge, he commented flatly, "Oh, you're from the *big* city." I wasn't sure if this was an observation or a judgment.

"Are you from around here?" I asked, returning the question to him.

"Nawh," he replied with a long pause. "I'm from Chrisney."

Chrisney is a little town *in the same county*, only about fifteen minutes south and west of where my property is located. Having thought that returning to southern Indiana in general had meant coming back home, I realized that from his perspective Evansville might as well have been California. In a place where local memory and geography are *so* local, I feared I might never fit in, or, in the words of author and geneticist Wes Jackson, become "native to this place."

The raising of the pole barn was, by turns, exhilarating, frustrating, and exhausting. Ever the perfectionist, I measured everything to the sixteenth of an inch and laid out stakes and strings to outline the shape of the building. I rented a power auger, and my dad, who would occasionally come out to work with me, helped bore perfect postholes in the parched, hard ground for the barn's support poles. I had arranged for a volunteer crew of my friends, my parents' friends, and even my father and stepfather together to come out the next day and help erect the frame.

As if in direct rebuke to my tendencies toward control, the skies opened that night and it rained several inches. When my crew and I arrived at the building site, it was a muddy swamp, and all of the four-foot-deep postholes were filled to the brim with mud and water.

Had I not been surrounded by all these other men, I would have cursed, cried, and probably given up. As I think back on such moments of being overwhelmed, which have been a fairly common occurrence in my life on this farm, I am beginning to see what an invaluable and necessary—though painful—lesson they have offered me about the limits of my ability to control every aspect of my life. Any bad habit dies hard, but among mine, I have found it particularly difficult to let go of the need to control, especially because American culture tends to encourage and reward what is essentially a personal pathology. And yet as those muddy, caved-in post holes signified, reality always wins—no matter how much energy one expends in asserting one's will against it.

One of the older, wiser men acknowledged this fact with a simple phrase. "What are you gonna do," he said, shaking his head, as if to say, "it figures!" It was a statement rather than a question, however, so what we were "gonna do" was simply get started and do the best we could. Though I chafed against it all day, my imagined standards of construction perfection were lowered to "good enough for a barn," and we got to work bailing out the soupy holes, setting the posts as best we could, and assembling the wall framing to hold everything together. My mom, God bless her, came out to cheer us on and keep us fed, cooking spaghetti on a camp stove perched on a truck tailgate.

A week or two later, I assembled pretty much the same crew to help set the barn's roof trusses. We got it done, and all in all, I was proud of the men in my crew and what we accomplished. We weren't Amish, most of the men were at least fifty to sixty years old, and only one of us had come from any sort of manual labor background. And yet we made it happen.

We finished the roof framing in a few hours without any broken trusses or broken bones. I couldn't stop looking up and marveling at the structure we'd created, which now finally had the skeletal but recognizable shape of a barn. I was humbled by the gift these men had given of their time and skill. I thanked all of them profusely, and while I could tell that they were glad to have done me a favor, they too felt immense satisfaction in what we had accomplished. Most of us came from professional backgrounds: management, finance, engineering, education, ministry, and so forth. So to gather around such a concrete project, I realized in my gratitude, was more than a kindness to me; it was a blessing to all of us. After the boom truck left and the stress and time pressure eased, we all sat around on the tailgates of our trucks, congratulating ourselves and regaling each other with stories of how it had gone.

To my mind, there was something undeniably good in what we had done together. We felt connected by that common work. I suppose, in other circumstances, we could have bonded with a lot of soul-baring talk, cathartic tears, and perhaps beating of drums. The unfortunate truth, however, is that it is difficult (and therefore very rare) for most men to connect with each other through honesty and vulnerability. My father and I rarely could when I was growing up. We communicated mainly by washing cars and running errands together. Even now, long after my childhood wounds have mostly healed over, we still have a limited emotional vocabulary with each other. And so it was with this group of mostly older men. We spoke the language we knew: of hammer, saw, and level. Truth has many pathways, and our truth was a structure now standing in the background.

As I continued to order the fields and build the barn, I looked for a day job to shore up my hemorrhaging bank account. In December, after several false and discouraging starts, I happened to hear about an open position at the Saint Meinrad School of Theology. I had assumed I would have at least an hour's commute to any job I could find, and yet Saint Meinrad, a Roman Catholic archabbey, seminary, and graduate school run by a large

Benedictine monastic community, was only fifteen easy miles from my farm. Although the job didn't light my fire or strike me as being something I would want to do for the rest of my life, its availability and proximity seemed serendipitous, especially given my past flirtation with the Catholic tradition. I was offered the job in mid-December, with a start date in mid-February, and I negotiated into my contract the free use of a dorm room until I was able to make the barn livable.

I had two months, then, to make as much progress as possible on the barn before a day job radically altered my daily routine. In this effort, my uncle Ron ended up being another angel. Not long after the roof-raising, we had a week in which we drove together out to the property every day at 6:00 a.m. and worked all day, finishing the details of the framing and screwing on large sheets of metal siding. Well into winter now, some mornings we had to chip ice off the roof purlins before we could nail down the insulation sheets and screw down the metal. The wind blew cold and insistently, sometimes threatening to catch the large metal sheets like a sail and send us flying off the roof. I was chilled through and through, but Ron, the veteran of working outdoors, nestled snugly (and smugly) in his Carhartt coveralls, which were faded almost white from repeated washings.

"What you need to do is get yourself a pair of Carhartts," he admonished me over and over. "You don't have any business farming if you don't have a pair of Carhartts."

He was right, of course, and my most treasured Christmas gift ever came that year: my very own Carhartt coveralls, with a matching jacket! I wore them like a badge of honor, like a new skin for a new life. Clothes do not make the man *per se*, but just as tattoos, piercings, and other changes of one's external appearance or clothing mark one as belonging to a particular group, I felt like Carhartts somehow helped me gain admission into some sort of special fraternity, especially once they started to look rather used. And, of course, they kept me warm. A decade later, I still have them, and I am proud of every stain, frayed edge, and tear.

By the time I began working at Saint Meinrad, I had the barn nearly completed, and I set to work preparing to pour the concrete slab for the apartment. Grateful for the six-month sojourn in my parents' basement but also eager to transplant my life closer to my property, I took up residence in a dorm room at Saint Meinrad.

This lasted only a few weeks, however. Having moved this close, I wanted desperately to live on the land I had already invested so much in. To my way of thinking, I had already completed a rudimentary form of shelter. Granted, I had no electricity, no heat, no plumbing or running water, and no phone. But at least I could stay dry. I figured that my simple living experiments in Atlanta, along with my backpacking and camping experience, had prepared me for roughing it. At the time I saw it as part and parcel of this grand adventure. I have come to believe, as Robert Bly puts it in *Iron John: A Book about Men*, that this offered me a chance to cultivate the "warrior spirit" in me in service of a greater cause. It was an ordeal, a way to toughen me up and help me earn the right to claim the new life I was trying to create for myself. And besides, I was operating with a net: if I found I couldn't hack it, I still had a dorm room to fall back on!

I set up camp in the barn on two four-by-eight-foot sheets of plywood, set off the barn's dirt floor with wooden pallets. On one end of my temporary home I set up my bedroom: an old cot with a sleeping bag. On the other end was my kitchen and study. An old door resting on sawhorses served as my desk, kitchen counter, and dining room table. I pulled out the two-burner camp stove I had used in Atlanta (a relic of my "unique" days of urban simple living) and I set up a slop sink fed by a plastic water jug I refilled at Saint Meinrad. For light I had a headlamp, flashlights, and my trusty kerosene lantern.

I kept my clothes in the dorm room at Saint Meinrad, and in the mornings I would shower and change there. When cleaning up at the farm, I used a "solar shower" designed for camping: a heavy plastic bag with a short hose and spout, which I would leave out in the sun to warm up and hoist up with a rope on the south side of the barn, offering me privacy from the road. In terms of relieving myself, I joked with friends and family that I had the largest bathroom of anyone I knew: twenty acres and a shovel.

Early March in southern Indiana is still very cool and perhaps not the most auspicious time to begin a camping adventure. Evenings I kept myself warm digging trenches for the concrete footer of the apartment floor slab and otherwise working on the apartment, but when I settled in to eat a late supper and read or journal by lamplight, the cold crept in with implacable insistence. I bundled up in layers, seeing my breath as I read or fumbling as I tried to hold a pen with heavy gloves. Often I went to bed early, simply for the warmth of my sleeping bag.

And so I went about my double life. By day, I worked a respectable office job interacting with a community of monks, faculty, and students who gave me, at the time an Episcopalian, a fascinating look into the inner world of Catholicism. By evening, early morning, and weekend, I did solitary manual labor and lived rough. For the most part, I shoved my loneliness to a back corner of my consciousness and tried to look on all these hardships as an adventure and a proving ground meant to test my mettle. I knew that my parents were quietly horrified at the living conditions their son had chosen. At times, I, too, was horrified, especially when I often heard mice scurrying at night beneath (and probably on top of) my plywood floor decking. Several nights I gave up, frigid and frustrated, and drove in late to my dorm room at Saint Meinrad, a warm, rodent-free bedroom with the luxury of electric lights.

March is not only a cold month but a dark one, especially in a barn with no windows or electric lighting, and I often felt myself slipping into a darkness of my own. I often felt bitter, tallying all I'd forfeited for the dream of a farming life: my friends in Atlanta, my community at Holy Comforter, a respectable teaching job, the one-time goal of a PhD and a university career. All of these I had traded for the chance to live with mice in a cold, unlighted barn on a patch of scrubby ground in southern Indiana. There was little romance in this, in any sense of the word. It seemed like a poor trade, indeed.

When I was ready to pour the concrete slab for the apartment, I called around to find someone nearby who could help with the pouring and finishing. I was given the name Paul Frey. Paul was a man who lived very close to my farm and, though I did not know it then, was someone who would become a vitally important, if sometimes complicated, part of my life. I called him and described the job, and he agreed to come over in the next few days and take a look.

Unlike my backhoe operator, Paul was from "around here": he and his wife, Becky, have a farm within a mile of his parents' home-place, his siblings, and one of his children. In his mid- to late-forties when I met him, Paul is a strong man with a full head of thick, wire-brush brown hair; a handsome, deeply lined, and weather-beaten face; and work-hardened hands as rough as sandpaper. Like my uncle Ron, he has worked hard—too hard—all his life, and it shows: though still very physically powerful, he looks tired; he moves as if he is carrying a great weight on his shoulders. Disinclined (or perhaps too ornery) to work for anyone else, Paul runs his own contracting and home repair business. Over the years, I have come to marvel at (and learn from) Paul's ability to fix, make, and do just about anything. I've also learned how to carefully navigate around his fiercely held opinions, mostly keeping silent or changing the subject when he gets a full head of steam behind his latest conspiracy theory about government bureaucrats, Wall Street fat cats, and big corporations.

Paul agreed to take on the work, and we arranged a time for the pour. When the day came, he arrived with two relatives who also did construction. Since the apartment was in the back corner of the barn where the cement truck's chute wouldn't reach, three of us set up an assembly line of several wheelbarrows to haul the concrete, load by load, back to the slab—all 80,000 pounds of it!

When we finished I was immensely proud of what the four of us had accomplished, but in contrast to the barn-building project, there was little end-of-the-day fanfare. Paul and his crew lacked the investment in the project that I had: for them, this was simply another job, similar to the one the day before and the day to come. This was no novelty to them; nor did they, also unlike my barn-raising crew, have enough personal connection with me to rejoice in it for my sake. Still, we all worked hard that day, and we took a moment at the end to congratulate ourselves and each other.

I felt like an outsider among these work-hardened men, and by day's end I was tired and sore. But I had held my own and, I must admit, was pleased by my ability to do so. As far as I could tell, Paul and his relatives had zero interest in whether I could expound on theological subtleties or whether I could honestly articulate my emotions or vulnerabilities; I quickly recognized that their measure of me was based almost entirely on how much work I could do in a day. While such a measure of a man is a very incomplete one, it was good to know that when pushed, I could do plenty, and for the most part, do it as quickly and well as they could.

Looking back on it now, I can see that day was about much more than laying concrete. With the benefit of time, a larger perspective, and being much more at peace with who I am now than at the beginning of my adventure, I see how insecure I was, how desperately I sought approval and acceptance from these men—and from my other mentors as well. Who doesn't, at least at some point in their development? Hauling concrete that day felt like something bigger than work. It felt like an important initiation rite. I was still discovering and forming who I was at that point; learning that I could work as hard as these experienced men became an important part of my self-confidence and my self-understanding. Was that a good thing? Did I really need to prevail in the face of insecurity about my "toughness" in order to let it go? Does being tough matter? I think that my answer to this question is "sometimes, yes." I suspect that, paradoxically, you sometimes have to prove yourself to discover that you don't have to prove yourself.

Soon the apartment was framed, and I was able to cut openings in the barn siding to install windows. After a few months of living in the darkness of the barn, the darkness of winter, and the emotional darkness of my mostly solitary work, the advent of natural light was nearly a religious experience. The days were getting longer, and the nights were not quite so chill as the farm woke up from its winter slumber. I could finally begin to see the world beyond the four metal walls of the barn's dark interior and take up in earnest my agricultural vocation.

That first year I put in a small garden patch on south-sloping ground just south of the barn. Still in my "purist" phase and as yet lacking the proper tillage equipment, I dug it by hand, loosening the soil deeply with a gardening fork, turning it with a spade, and breaking up the clods with rake and hoe. After the hammer-banging, circular-sawing, and generator-running noisiness of much of the apartment construction, this was blessedly quiet, wonderfully centering outdoor work, work that reminded me of why I chose this life in the first place. With little at my disposal in terms of organic fertilizers or soil amendments, that first garden would do predictably poorly that season, but well enough to provide some fresh produce. More importantly, it fed my desire to grow things and fueled my hope that the next season would be even better.

The rest of the year was a three-fold balancing act between a full-time job at Saint Meinrad, tending the small garden and improving the larger fields, and finishing the apartment. I abandoned my two-plywood-sheet bivouac and moved in. I gave up the cot for a double bed and even added a dresser and some other honest-to-goodness furniture from my parents' attic.

In spite of contending with mice and now mosquitoes and other insects in the warming weather, in spite of still lacking electricity, refrigeration, climate control, or plumbing, my living conditions began to feel like some shade of civilized. When I finally installed the bathroom tub, I was even able to bring in my five-gallon solar shower bag, hang it on a nail above the not-yet-functional showerhead, and savor several minutes' worth of indoor bathing with warm water.

My months of rough living gave me a small sense of solidarity with those in poor nations, so it was with some ambivalence that I slowly regained many of the luxuries I had once taken for granted. What I tried to do after stripping my comforts and conveniences back to practically nothing, however, was regain them in a new, more sustainable way. After a good deal of thinking and much research, for example, I bit the bullet and followed through with my decision to avoid using utility power, investing several thousand dollars in a power system where a rack of roof-mounted solar panels charged a big bank of heavy-duty golf cart batteries I kept in a bathroom closet.

The day I did the final connections and got the system working was one of the true early triumphs on the farm. I threw the breaker, heard the power inverter start humming, and watched the lights come on, running entirely on solar power: by some technological miracle, the light of the sun was captured and reproduced in those little compact fluorescent bulbs. To know that my power was independent of the pollution and control of the coal-burning utility company was a source of great satisfaction (and a little self-righteousness). But I also had some misgivings. Even the soft hums of the inverter and—finally!—a dorm-sized refrigerator felt like an intrusion into what had previously been almost complete silence. I missed the soulfulness of lamplight as well. I was seeking a simpler life, yet here I was installing high-tech, computerized equipment, the inner workings of which were a complete mystery to me. My consolation was that it met my criteria for what "good" technology should be: equipment that was designed to create non-polluting, renewable energy, and which made me *more* aware of the natural world, not less, since my household electricity supply now depended on sunlight. I never looked at weather and seasons in the same way again. The sun, when it shone, was that much more of a gift. Cloudy days and shorter winter days were days of careful—even stingy—energy conservation.

To avoid the considerable expense of running a water line and to stay independent of the county water company, I built a small cistern to collect rainwater from the barn roof and rigged up pumps and filters to supply all my household water needs. It worked well, but without a lot of storage capacity, I would learn to be very careful about how much I watered the gardens, how long I showered, and when I did laundry. I found that if I was conservative in my use of water and electricity, I had enough. Not too much extra, but enough—which, like our daily bread, is all anyone can rightly ask for. All of it is a gift, freely given by a generous natural world and its generous God.

By this point it was deep into November, more than a year since I'd bought the property, and the apartment was getting decidedly cool. In order to deal with the cold without the benefit of a dorm room to retreat to, I rigged up an old salvaged woodstove. It worked well—too well, in fact. On the first night of its operation, I woke up sweating in a 95-degree apartment, frantic I'd set the place on fire. Over that winter I would slowly learn the art of maintaining a woodstove so as to keep the apartment at a reasonable temperature. Like the power and water systems, wood heat and a passive-solar home demanded that I pay attention: to the current weather, the forecast, the type of wood I was burning. In all this, I came to love heating with wood, a once-common practice that has become a rare privilege in an increasingly urbanized society. It was a thrill to stay warm without paying a heating bill, and this was yet another way to provide for my own needs from my own land. There is something wonderfully elemental and romantic about the cutting, hauling, splitting, stacking, and burning of wood. My body, which otherwise sat at a desk many hours of the day, reveled in that hard work and its tangible results. I loved the feast wood heat provided for the senses: the sound of a fire crackling at first then roaring with good draft; the sight of well-stacked cordwood and the mesmerizing dance of flame in the stove's belly; the scent of wood smoke; the encompassing warmth that no electric or gas furnace can possibly replicate.

A year and a few months since purchasing my land, I felt like I was finally settling in. The fields were cleaned up, smoothed out, and neatly mowed; I had raised a small garden, I was getting to know my land, and I had a place to live. Granted, my kitchen was still a door on sawhorses with a camp-stove; my toilet was still a trip outside or a lidded bucket as a chamber pot; my only hot water came from a camp-shower bag left in the sun, and my apartment was still unpainted and had a bare concrete floor. But my home was dry and warm, and I had electricity and running water. At the dawn of the twenty-first century, I was already edging past the nineteenth and entering the twentieth! Although I was still mostly a stranger in the neighborhood, I was beginning to know my neighbors, and I could at least imagine fitting in some day. In spite of a year of rough living and overwork, by most measures I was happy and satisfied with my new life.

No good life is without its costs, however. As I entered my second winter back in Indiana and the pace of my work slackened a bit, the solitary nature of my experience became all the more clear to me. I came to realize that the downside of my desire for "independent living" was that on a certain level I had set myself up for a hermit's life. Be careful of what you wish for; you might get it! I did love solitude; I was neither depressed nor utterly bereft of company, and I was not consumed by thoughts of companionship. I loved growing closer to my parents and developing our relationship on adult terms. I was slowly getting to know people at Saint Meinrad and elsewhere, and with letters and phone calls and occasional visits, I maintained older friendships. Nonetheless, in my few idle moments, especially in my journaling and in prayer, a sense of loneliness seeped through the hustle and bustle. Even as I worked hard to become as independent as I could in terms of my basic material needs, I realized how worthless a goal it would be if it came at the expense of personal relationships. I wasn't cut out to be a hermit. I longed for meaningful community.

chapter three

Loneliness and Love

With no right to expect it, in my more honest moments I still yearned for a family to share what was unfolding on the farm. This was problematic in that the chances of meeting a woman willing to share my "basic" lifestyle, much less meeting her in a sparsely populated rural area, were fairly slim. To make matters worse, I was insanely busy with building, and most of the people I encountered on a daily basis at Saint Meinrad were celibate monks and priests. This problem was brought home all too clearly for me in a conversation I had with a local woman who cuts my hair.

Martha knew the entire county's business inside and out, and delighted in sharing it as she clipped away. During my very first haircut with her, Martha got around to asking me about my marital status, and I admitted that I was single but looking for a relationship. As I did so, I felt a faint rise of hope that this woman, who knew everyone, might relish the role of matchmaker.

"You're a good-looking-enough guy," she said, ceasing her cutting to step back and appraise me. "How old are you, anyway?"

"Twenty-seven," I replied, trying to sound nonchalant and non-desperate.

"Oh," she replied, returning to her work with a sigh of finality. "It's over for you."

I offered a feeble protest. "What do you mean?"

"Well, in this county, there aren't nearly enough good women for the men who are looking," she explained. "And once a woman gets to your age, she's either left or gotten married, or both."

"Oh."

"Well, maybe you can try to place an ad or something?"

I agreed, if only as a desperate attempt to stop this conversation before I felt even more pathetic. Realizing that Martha had a point about the dearth of romantic opportunity in the local community, over the next year or so I made a few efforts to start or rekindle long-distance relationships. One attempt in particular not only fizzled but laid bare a real problem in terms of finding someone with whom to make a life together.

For a short time, I reconnected with a woman I had met in Atlanta while I was teaching a summer theology program. At the time, our age difference kept the relationship platonic, but by this point Sheila was a junior at the University of Notre Dame, involved in the Catholic Worker movement, and living a mere six hours away—all of which I rather immaturely took as a divine mandate for romance.

We'd kept in touch for a few years by letter, connected by our common interests in spirituality, social justice, and sustainable agriculture. When I began establishing the farm, our correspondence picked up. She came to visit that first fall, camping with me on the property, and sparks flew. Soon we were writing letters almost daily and telephoning frequently. I reveled vicariously in what she was learning in her theology classes, in her experiences with the Catholic Worker community in South Bend, in the various movements and protests in which she took part. I visited her up at Notre Dame, and at least in my eyes, our future looked exciting and rosy. For me, having been drawn for years to Catholicism and its synthesis of sacramental imagination with active social engagement, her deep commitment to faith and social justice activism was an irresistible combination. I fell in love.

Things ended with a painful jolt, however. We traveled to Fort Benning, Georgia, that November, taking part in the large annual "School of the Americas Watch" protest of the military installation there. Unexpectedly—at least to me—she explained, in a few curt sentences, that she felt more drawn to a life of activism and radical witness, perhaps as a vowed religious, than she did to our romantic relationship.

I made my way home from the event, grateful to be back but brokenhearted and feeling lonelier and lower than I could remember. I realized it was not just the loss of the relationship that had deflated me, but also the nagging doubt that perhaps the life I had chosen, a life of settledness and stability, was too tame, too unexciting, too pedestrian. Were truly radical Christians the ones who, like Jesus, had no place to lay their head, who were unattached to possessions and places such that they could go wherever the action was? Was the desire for home an illusion, or worse, a betrayal of true Christian faith?

Solvitur ambulando: "It is solved by walking." I did not have ready answers to these questions, but I did have plenty of work to do. Staying busy helped me to work through my disappointment and dashed hopes, or at least keep me distracted from them. But the work itself also became an answer of sorts, for on some fundamental level I experienced it as good and meaningful work: tangible, concrete actions that brought daily challenges and satisfactions, and which, I hoped, helped to make at least one small corner of the world better than I found it.

The fact of my aloneness, however, was never far from my consciousness. It felt like a slight limp, which did not slow me down much but served to remind me that I did not feel quite whole. With some fear and trembling, I decided that for the time being, I should give up on my search for companionship. I had to accept, or at least try to accept, that the life choice I had made might prevent me from finding a partner. In order to keep working, I had to make some sort of reconciliation within myself, putting my agrarian convictions on a balance against my romantic aspirations and realizing that if I could not have both, the former outweighed the latter: my primary vocation lay in the life and location I was consciously choosing anew every day. I had to be faithful to that, and let the romantic chips fall where they would.

Even after making this decision, though, I found that I had to make it again and again. Too often I caught myself in the middle of a project, such as cutting firewood or mowing a field, daydreaming that I was doing the task to please some imagined wife. There was a certain sweetness to such thoughts of conjured domesticity. But they placed an unreasonable measure against my life as it really was. I realized that if I always viewed what I was doing in light of the lack of a life partner or the dream of her arrival, my chosen life would always come up short, and I would miss the many gifts that my life was able to offer as it was, rather than as I dreamed it should be. It became a bit of a spiritual discipline for me to embrace and befriend my solitude, not just as a cross to bear, but as a kind of companion in and of itself.

Of course, I never completely reconciled myself to the idea of a life without a wife and family. And even if I had, I'm highly doubtful as to whether I would have wanted to move to the point of renunciation of that desire. Human beings are made for community, to know and be known intimately. Even a celibate is still a sexual person—and should be. Several of my monk friends have told me that they still struggle, even after years of living in community, to be reconciled to their aloneness. I love them for it. This struggle is part of what keeps them fully alive and fully human. I've yet to meet (nor would I want to) anyone who has managed to extinguish completely the desire for community and intimacy. In retrospect, I think, it was my inability to be fully reconciled to the single life that kept me open to the opportunity to embrace love when its possibility appeared in an unlikely form.

In the meantime, however, the lack of a partner led me to embrace other loves and other communities. My celibate colleagues and friends at Saint Meinrad taught me that one of the great gifts of celibacy is the constant invitation it provides to share one's love in wider circles than just one's partner or immediate family. In the monastery, the healthy monk sublimates his sexual desire and translates it into passion for his prayer, his work, and the life in community with his brothers. I have seen how celibate priests with healthy boundaries and well-integrated sexuality are available to minister to their parish communities with a devotion that I think would be far more challenging if they were trying at the same time to juggle the concerns and responsibilities of their own family.

Through taking up a "vocation of location," I began to see the land itself as a sort of spouse—although the commitment, to be sure, more resembled an arranged marriage. I had paid my dowry and signed a contract, and now we were getting to know each other and figuring out how to live with one another. As I got to know the farm better, however, I felt a real shift in my thinking, one from ownership and an abstract ideal of responsibility to a deeper, more personal, even tender connection. I began to care about, not just to care for, this particular piece of land.

I had pledged fidelity to the land, for better and for worse. As experience shifted my thinking from the ideas of "field" and "woods" to *this* field and *these* woods, the farm revealed itself to me, as a spouse might, in ways both wonderful and difficult. I began to learn where the soil was eroded and exhausted or deep and fertile, where the sandy loam drained well and the heavy clay lay wet. In the woodlot, I began to discover the black walnuts and their green-globed gifts in the fall; the shagbark and slickbark hickories, which split easily and burned hot in the woodstove—and the elms, which didn't; the few old black cherry and tulip poplar trees that somehow escaped the chainsaw and whose girth I couldn't get my arms halfway around (though like a true tree-hugger, I tried). I saw the unkindness of lightning strikes and strong winds, the slow-healing scars of poor logging, the valiant and doomed struggle of trees against disease or the life-choking shade of a closing forest canopy. I learned that the land had its own life and its own freedom, which, as often as not, failed to conform to my wishes.

Good relationships are those in which "iron sharpens iron": where partners help each other grow and change for the better. I began to believe deeply in what the farm could become with good work and devotion, and what I could become in providing them. And although I had chosen the land, I got to the point of wondering if, in some mysterious way, the land had also somehow chosen me. I came across a short story of Wendell Berry's, "It Wasn't Me," in which the character Wheeler Catlett helped to name something of what I was feeling:

> The land expects something from us. The line of succession, the true line, is the membership of people who know it does. . . . We start out expecting things of it. All of us do, I think. And then some of us, if we stay put and pay attention, see that expectations are going the other way too. Demands are being made of us, whether we know it or not. The place is crying out to us to do better, to be worthy of it.[1]

In moments of ignorance and impatience, I often felt far from worthy of my land and its expectations. But I also had a sense that, like any good marriage, my relationship with the land rested ultimately on a kinder foundation than what it demanded and expected of me, or I of it. As I did my imperfect best with the few skills and little knowledge I had, as I committed always to do better, I sensed not only the land's expectations, but also its long, gentle patience and deep, divinely rooted forgiveness. Love was what bound us together: the love of the Creator, encompassing and sustaining all of Creation.

A wife and children were not the only family I sought, and trading my dreams of academe and accomplishment for a much less outwardly impressive life on the land was not the only leap of faith I made in settling on a small farm in southern Indiana. I also made another, more literal leap of faiths: from the Episcopal Church into the large, fascinating, and strange world of Roman Catholicism.

On one level, I suppose one could view my religious journey — time spent exploring Presbyterian, Methodist, Evangelical, Catholic, Lutheran, Hindu, Zen Buddhist, and Episcopal traditions — as that of a "cafeteria Christian" or an attention-deficit dilettante, unwilling to make a lasting commitment to any particular tradition. Looking back now, however, after over a decade of being Catholic, I have come to see that journey less as dabbling or window shopping and more as a search that kept drawing me ever closer to a tradition in which I could truly belong for the long haul. In some sense, finally becoming Catholic was yet another homecoming, of a piece with settling on the farm.

If pressed, I could cough up a long list of reasons why I was drawn to the Catholic tradition. The philosopher and theologian in me, ever on the search for both meaningful answers and challenging questions, admired the reasoned solidity of Catholic doctrine (even when I struggled to accept it) and the two-millennia-long tradition of reflection from which it emerged. As a moral idealist, I especially appreciated its coherent and far-reaching ethical teaching and the grit and pluck with which Catholic organizations, such as Catholic Charities, Catholic Relief Services, and many others, were applying its principles in the most dire situations and the most devastated places on Earth. A lover of beauty, I appreciated the Catholic sacramental imagination, which affirmed the world and sought the glory of God in it. I admired the magnificent architecture of the cathedrals Catholics had erected, and even the shrines to the confusing panoply of Catholic saints—including, of course, the near-omnipresent Virgin Mother.

I also began to realize that almost all of the authors whose thought had shaped mine or whose lives I especially admired were Catholic. Through his writings, I followed Thomas Merton's path from skepticism and doubt to fanatic enthusiasm for Catholicism and monastic life, to his mature struggles and curiosity about the linkages between Christian and Eastern contemplative traditions. I resonated with the mystical wisdom of Meister Eckhart and Julian of Norwich, and Thérèse of Lisieux. I cheered the doggedly strong devotion of Dorothy Day and Peter Maurin, who founded the Catholic Worker movement of justice-oriented intentional communities. I savored the powerful prose of G. K. Chesterton and Annie Dillard and the unforgettable characters crafted by novelists Graham Greene, Walker Percy, and Flannery O'Connor. I cogitated on Teilhard de Chardin, Karl Rahner, Thomas Aquinas, and other Catholic intellectual giants. Even reading the economist

E. F. Schumacher helped me to realize how deeply the Catholic tradition had influenced his thought.

Few religious conversions, however, begin or end solely in the intellect. Finally, it was my direct experience of Catholicism that drew me "home to Rome." The seeds had been planted by a friend and mentor from college and the time I had spent worshipping at the Newman Center on the Indiana University campus. They finally germinated when I returned to Indiana.

While still living with my parents and commuting to the farm, I sought out a very special Catholic parish in downtown Evansville, St. Mary's. This fascinating community, profiled in a recent publication as one of three hundred especially vibrant parishes in the United States, paradoxically combined the very ornate, traditional architecture of its almost 150-year-old sanctuary with a congregation well known for its diversity, its lively liturgies, and its active engagement with social justice issues.

The parishioners at St. Mary's welcomed me warmly. Feeling like such an awkward novice in so many other areas of my life, I experienced St. Mary's as a place where I could belong without any pretense. I decided to go through the Rite of Christian Initiation for Adults (RCIA), the inquiry and formation process for adults to join the Catholic Church—not because I had decided on converting, but as a way to grow more connected to the community there, and to discern whether Catholicism might indeed be the religious home for which I'd long been searching. This helped me become better acquainted with the Catholic tradition, but far more importantly, it led me to worship in a Catholic community. As when I'd worshipped with my disabled friends at Holy Comforter in Atlanta, I felt a strong anchoring in liturgy and ritual that engaged my body and its various senses rather than just my head, and in so doing, allowed my faith to rest on more than just the sometimes-shaky foundation of my beliefs. As at Holy Comforter,

I felt myself part of a close-knit community, but one that at the same time felt connected to a greater whole and had wide, deep roots in a much larger, older, many-faceted tradition.

Not too many months after entering the RCIA process, I began my new job at Saint Meinrad. If through the RCIA at St. Mary's I had cautiously dipped my toe in the water of Catholicism, beginning work at a Benedictine monastery and school of theology was like falling into the deep end of the pool. Saint Meinrad was founded more than 150 years ago by monks from the Swiss Abbey of Einsiedeln, with a mission of starting a school to train German-speaking priests who would minister to the many German Catholic immigrants in this region of southern Indiana. The handsome sandstone buildings of Saint Meinrad are massive and medieval-looking, their thick-walled architecture bespeaking the solid continuity of the 1,500-year Benedictine monastic tradition.

The campus sits atop a hill among the rolling fields and woodlands of the surrounding rural area, and underneath all the busyness of the various programs and visiting groups, it has a quiet, purposeful peace grounded in the monastic community's daily faithfulness to their life of prayer. Now my weekdays were spent in the company of black-robed monks who had devoted their lives to the communal pursuit of sanctity, as well as priests, students, faculty, and staff whose common mission was ministry and service in the Catholic Church. It was a head-snapping culture shock compared to the frenetic urban jungle in which I had lived just six months earlier.

Although in some sense I did "convert" to Catholicism, I also converted to Catholics themselves. As I got to know individual Catholics at Saint Meinrad, St. Mary's, and elsewhere, I came to the paradoxical realization that this tradition of lofty, almost otherworldly mystics and monks, of often obsessive guilt about all things sexual and bodily, at the same time harbored people whose faith somehow helped them be more fully themselves, rather than less, and more fully engaged with the world, rather than less. The earthy, unapologetic humanness of the monks and other Catholics I encountered, far from scandalizing me, was actually a great relief. Here was a tradition in which I needn't check myself, my loves, and my faults at the door. Here was a tradition in which I could strive with others for heaven even as we embraced an imperfect life in the good, grounded gift of Creation. So at the Easter Vigil in the Jubilee Year of 2000, I was received into full communion with the wild, wonderful family that is the Roman Catholic Church. In a place far deeper than my mind, I felt that I had finally found home.

Love often arrives when you are least prepared for it, and in a way you least expect. More than a year into my new life on the farm, as I was busy rigging up solar panels on my unfinished bachelor-pad apartment, I met a Louisville priest, Fr. Joe Merkt, at a day-long meeting for Saint Meinrad. I joined him and several others for lunch, during which we each shared a bit about ourselves, and at the close of the meeting, bade him farewell without much more thought.

A few days later, however, I received a strange note from him. I sat befuddled in my office at Saint Meinrad, learning that he knew a young woman named Cyndi who shared similar interests and values with me, and with whom he thought I might connect well and forge a friendship. Bewildered that this man I barely knew might be trying to set me up, I called him to find out what I could.

Fr. Joe laughed a bit ruefully when he took my call. "I don't often do much matchmaking," he admitted. "I don't even know if you're attached, or gay, or even looking. But the whole time I was with you at lunch the other day, I couldn't get Cyndi out of my mind. I think at the very least, you two could be great friends."

Fr. Joe and I agreed to meet for dinner in Louisville a few days later, where he explained things more fully. Fr. Joe had been childhood friends with Cyndi's mother Barbara in Louisville, and they had stayed in touch over the years. When as a young adult Cyndi had made her way from her family's home in western Pennsylvania to Louisville, Barbara had contacted Fr. Joe and asked him to "keep an eye on her." He became a mentor and a wise friend, who patiently listened and counseled, helping Cyndi do some healing work and grapple with religious questions regarding the Catholic tradition in which she had been raised.

Having grown up on a small farm similar to the one I was trying to create, Cyndi was an artist and singer with a deep love of nature, animals, and growing things. After a long period of spiritual searching, with Fr. Joe's help she had rediscovered an open-minded and open-hearted side of Catholicism, and finally reclaimed her childhood faith on her own terms. Cyndi tried, as I also did, to connect her spirituality with her love of Creation, and had also dreamed of having a small farm on which to do so. Fr. Joe wasn't halfway through his soliloquy when I had a strong, gut-level feeling that his instincts were right. Cyndi had since relocated from Louisville to Raleigh, North Carolina, so Fr. Joe and I agreed that he would let her know about our conversation, and that I would be in touch with a letter.

Despite that initial feeling, it took me six weeks to gather enough courage to write a letter to a total stranger about whom I knew so little and whose appearance a sixty-plus-year-old celibate priest had merely described as "dark-haired and attractive." I worked on it evening after evening, writing by kerosene lantern with a quill pen and inkpot, flummoxed at how best to describe myself and my life and inquire about her and hers. I wrote entirely too much, finally called it done, and sent the letter on its way with a nervous, hopeful prayer.

A few weeks later a small envelope arrived with C. Matous on the return address. With a pounding heart and a queasy stomach, I opened it to find a beautiful hand-made card with an exquisite, brilliantly-colored mandala on the cover. With spare, careful, almost calligraphied prose, Cyndi had responded to my questions, and posed her own. She described her family members in some detail, in a way that revealed they were a large part of her consciousness. She explained that she had moved to Raleigh not with ambitious career plans, but simply to be nearer the ocean, for which she had a deep love, and to decompress from several intense years in Louisville, during which time she had worked with disabled adults in a residential facility and cared for her dying aunt.

Thus began our slow, cautious exchange of letters. As we shared our stories and our dreams, I could tell Cyndi was strong-minded, but not in the same driven, goal-oriented, approval-seeking way that I was. She, too, felt passionately about what values made for a worthwhile life, but she had lived her passion by serving others and by cultivating her interior life more than pursuing professional or academic ambitions. I realized that I, who lived largely out of my head and its plans and projects, had a lot to learn from someone like Cyndi. I began to hope that she, too, might find our differences redemptive.

I found myself, then, cultivating feelings about a woman I had never met, spoken with, or even seen in a picture. I finally enclosed a few shots of myself and my family in one of my letters and asked if she might consider doing the same. Among the photos of her parents and six siblings she included in her next letter, Cyndi sent two of herself: one as a three-year-old girl with her farmer/nuclear physicist father as he was building the family's house (to convince me that she, too, was an experienced carpenter), and another of her as an adult: a beautiful, green-eyed woman with fair skin and thick, dark hair, sitting on a tire swing in Raleigh's large botanical garden. I began to wish I'd had a better haircut in my own photos!

Something shifted with our exchange of pictures. It made what had been somewhat abstract seem much more real, and consequently, what had been cautiously platonic started to feel a lot more like romance. The months passed and we continued our letters, and when Valentine's Day approached, I struggled with how to give a gift to a woman I'd never met and whom I was not officially dating. I finally had delivered to her a small pot of blooming purple hyacinth bulbs, and not too long afterward I received a card on which Cyndi had reproduced them in colored pencil as her way of saying thanks. Shortly thereafter, I cautiously asked whether we might continue our letters but also try more frequent contact by e-mail. Cyndi agreed, and for several more months we traded e-mails regularly, in which we shared much more of the daily and mundane parts of our lives—the stuff of which real life and real relationships are largely composed. Finally, I invited her to visit, and she agreed to come out in early spring.

I panicked about this, not just at the thought of meeting her, but because I realized that while my half-finished apartment was a far cry from the days of sleeping bags and mice, it was also a far cry from anything a woman in her right mind would find appealing. I was still using what was basically a chamber pot and was planning to install an honest-to-goodness composting toilet. My mother had pointed out repeatedly (and unbidden) that shared values or not, no sane woman would tolerate either. I was determined not to blow my rare romantic opportunity, so with the help of a few friends and neighbors with plumbing skills, I frantically got to work retrofitting a flush toilet. In my heretofore bull-headed insistence on a composting toilet, I had neglected to lay sewer lines when pouring the concrete floor. So I was forced to build a raised platform to provide clearance, thus giving the toilet a dramatic, throne-like appearance—an irony I didn't fail to notice. That blessed first flush occurred only a few days prior to Cyndi's arrival, and though the apartment still had no permanent kitchen, no paint, no hot water, and a bare concrete floor, it still felt like the Ritz Carlton to me.

When I arrived in Louisville to pick Cyndi up and take her out to the farm, I was mortified to discover that I had forgotten about the different time zone and was more than an hour late. As we hugged and I recovered from my embarrassment, I had the strange experience of falling in love with someone whom I had never seen and who at the same time felt like an old friend. As in her letters, Cyndi was soft-spoken but self-assured, gentle but intense. When we finally got back to the farm, I showed her around with great trepidation, for since my life was so firmly settled there, the question was not only if she could come to love me, but also if she could love the place itself. I nervously asked her what she thought of it, and with a long, careful look over the fields, the trees, and me, she replied simply, "It's beautiful, Kyle." With those few words I knew without a doubt that God had indeed called us together. The cold shower, the rough and unfinished apartment, my multitude of shortcomings, even the towering toilet— none of these could possibly stand in the way of our love.

The ensuing months were a blur. I flew out to visit Cyndi in Raleigh, and as our relationship grew more serious, she eventually decided to move back to Louisville. After that we saw each other each weekend, and she joined in the work of finishing the apartment. I traveled with Cyndi to meet her large family at her parents' farm in the mountains of western Pennsylvania. Her parents were gracious and courteous, and the several siblings who were there when I visited welcomed me warmly. Coming as I did from a family with only one sister, it took a while to get used to a house full of people and noise. In a strange way, though, I found I liked it—probably as a counterbalance to the long hours of silence on my farm.

The Matous family home-place was a lovely hillside farm, carefully situated amidst a difficult terrain of steep slopes and rocky soil, where over the years they had raised any number of crops and livestock. I could see how much care and attention had been lavished on it over the decades and how many memories had been made there. Cyndi took me around to many different parts of it, showing me where she and her sisters had had tea parties, picked blackberries and grapes and blueberries, ridden horses, and been terrorized by various mad roosters. She showed me how her father, a man of science and sensibility, had taken the time to create flower gardens, arbors, benches, and places of repose all around the farm, many of which included little ponds and pump-driven waterfalls and fountains. I realized it was from him that she had inherited much of her artistic instinct.

We hiked up to the top of "Old Roundtop," the mountain on whose side her family farm perched. "This is where I always did my best praying," she confessed, explaining that her spirituality was nurtured more by moonlight and mountains than by their small parish church, where every Sunday Cyndi's father and mother had always marched the family in like little soldiers and lined them up in the front pew. When she left her home town after studying art and family development at the university where her father taught, Cyndi also left the Catholic church for years, coming back only when Fr. Joe convinced her that under its wide umbrella there was room for her nature-inspired spirituality and her "hilltop God."

It was also at Cyndi's home-place that she agreed to marry me. When we returned we began meeting regularly with Fr. Joe for marriage preparation, in which he helped us articulate the values of faith, Creation care, creativity, and hospitality that we wanted as the bedrock of our marriage. With the help of a local artist, we tried to make our own wedding rings, carving them out of wax in order to make a mold that would cast them in gold. After he stood us up several times, and a second artist also fell through, we finally gave up. I suppose we could have taken this as a bad omen, but as Cyndi has often reminded me, this debacle foreshadowed an important truth about our marriage. It would not be easy or storybook perfect, but redemption could always follow disaster if we held on to each other and to the common purpose we sought for our life together. We ended up buying simple, matching gold bands, whose lack of ostentation spoke to our desire for beauty in simplicity. They also made sense because we anticipated a lifestyle that was sure to be hard on fancy rings.

We had a simple, inexpensive, homespun wedding in May, in the busy season of planting crops and cultivating weeds. Unable to be away from the farm for long, we spent a three-day mini-honeymoon at a friend's log cabin in Kentucky, and then we got to work together, settling into a new, shared home economy. Cyndi set the apartment to rights and started taking summer courses toward a theology degree at Saint Meinrad. Only about two weeks into our marriage, in conjunction with Saint Meinrad's retreat center, we led a three-day ecology and spirituality retreat. The retreatants were an eclectic group including Catholics of all stripes and sexual orientations, a Wiccan priestess, and a Baptist minister: a combination we feared would be explosive. But as we shared in each other's stories, explored our farm, and together planted the orchard trees we had received as wedding gifts, I saw how the grounding of a place and good, common work could draw people together despite their vast differences. What we experienced among the retreatants was also, I hoped, a precedent for how our marriage would unfold.

chapter four

Building Home

It is one of God's great mercies that with any great endeavor, be it a marriage, parenthood, or building a house, we cannot foresee exactly how things will turn out. Otherwise, most of us would likely succumb to a terrified paralysis and do nothing much at all. With blessed ignorance, Cyndi and I set about making a life together.

Accustomed to living lean, Cyndi brought blessedly little by way of furniture and possessions into our marriage, but even so, the barn apartment quickly became quite snug. As newlyweds, we found the close quarters more romantic than annoying, and we knew that even these accommodations were spacious and luxurious compared to those in the developing world. Besides, with all of the outdoor work to be done, we didn't plan to spend a lot of time inside, anyway. But about eight months after our wedding, when Cyndi started feeling sluggish and two pink stripes appeared on a pregnancy test, I panicked at the thought of adding a third occupant to our cramped abode. Just as we were nailing in the last few pieces of trim in the barn apartment, we decided that we should start planning a larger, permanent home. I recalled wryly the poet David Whyte, who once reflected that living authentically entails always being called to new, ever-larger houses of belonging—even as we're just settling in and getting comfortable. In our case, this became more than just a metaphor.

I found myself strangely unnerved at the thought of building a home. Despite my commitment to the farm and the area, despite that I'd already built one structure on it, to build the home in which we hoped to grow old felt like a terrifyingly irrevocable commitment to this location. Once I invested as much of myself as I knew it would take to build a home, I was sure I would be loathe to leave it.

I also could not see any way around a mortgage. Up to this point I had worked hard in order to avoid any debt whatsoever, trying my best to preserve the freedom to live simply. Harnessing myself to years of house payments—and the need to earn the steady income those payments would require—felt like apostasy from my simple living credo. Even today I feel ambivalent about it, but I have also begun to see that many of my early ideals of simplicity and independence had been fairly unrealistic—sometimes even immature and a bit selfish. Part of true adulthood—and true freedom—entails taking on responsibilities one cannot and would not abandon. I could not walk away from a mortgage and a half-built house any more than I could abandon our child that was on its way. Fatherhood and "builderhood" weighed equally heavy upon me, even as I realized that they were the necessary next steps. To take them meant to trust that this dreamed-of life was solid enough to hold them, and that these were steps not into slavery, but a new, more mature kind of freedom.

My concerns were not only commitment, money, and responsibility, however. I had built a barn and an apartment, and while they helped to hone my construction skills, they also showed me how complicated and challenging house-building really is and what a novice I was at it. Thousands of mistakes could be made during construction that would likely bring about a home's ruin.

Though wildly underestimating the amount of time and energy building our home would eventually demand of me, I had enough of an inkling even then to be daunted. Yet to have the kind of "green" home we wished for, and to afford it on one moderate income, I had little choice but to do almost all of the labor myself. I sought out our neighbor Paul once more, told him about our plans, and asked him, more or less, if he would have my back: if I could hire him as I might have need, or go to him with questions and problems as they arose. His willingness to help, and my trust in his knowledge and skill, set my mind at ease enough to move forward.

One of the most exhilarating and terrifying aspects of building was beginning with a blank slate. Whatever we ended up building would be, for better and worse, exactly what we dreamed up. Cyndi and I made a list of everything we wanted in a home, from aesthetics to environmental considerations. As with the apartment, we wanted a home attuned to its environment, depending on the sun, wind, woods, and rain for its power, heat, and water supply. The "small is beautiful" idea had lost some of its allure in our cramped apartment, so we desired a house that, while not oversized by American standards, was still spacious enough for a growing family and others who might stay with us.

We wanted a solid, durable home that would withstand the ravages of time, weather, and young children. We hoped to create a place of beauty, with sturdy, handsome materials and skilled, detailed workmanship, the kind of work common in the Arts-and-Crafts bungalows we so admired. With this list in mind, I found my old drafting board, T-square, and triangles from middle-school drafting class, and for months we drew and redrew plans. Though a visual person in many ways, it took a long time before Cyndi could look at a floor plan and imagine what the space would look like.

It took an even longer time for us to learn how to negotiate our respective priorities for the house. The apartment had been so much easier to design, not only because it was smaller and simpler, but because I had done it myself. Now partnered, difficult compromises had to be made.

We finally crafted a basic plan with which we were pleased, and we ran it past an architect friend, who gave her approval. The evening before the excavator was to arrive to dig the basement and a nearby pond, however, Cyndi had a few inspired ideas that required a total redesign with a completely different floor plan. I frantically redrew things, and even as the excavator unloaded his equipment, I was running around in a panic, changing marker flags to delineate the new footprint of the house.

Any builder would have laughed at the prospect of building a house from the limited (and last-minute) drawings we had sketched out for an L-shaped ranch house with a walk-out basement: a basic floor plan for the upstairs and another for the down, each on a single sheet typing of paper, with no section or elevation drawings, no wiring, plumbing, framing, or roofing diagrams. To go forward with such skimpy plans was a fool's errand, and we were fools. In some sense, though, who isn't? I have met very few people who have detailed designs for their lives, and the ones who do generally see them collapse—or else create misery for themselves and others by trying to impose them on uncooperative circumstances. Life is a generally messy process of improvising; our house-building process followed suit.

Cyndi's and my negotiation in the design phase was only the beginning of a long series of uneasy compromises our house-building entailed, not just with each other, but with our principles and ideals. After several years of living "off the grid," either going without electricity or generating it from solar panels and a windmill, we could not afford the investment in additional solar panels and other equipment required by the extra loads of a larger house. Chastened with trepidation and regret, I called the utility company and had a power line run to the farm. This not only added another regular payment on top of the mortgage, along with the lack of independence that implied, but also represented a new and uncomfortable complicity in the pollution spewing from the coal-fired power plants in this area and the strip-mined land that supplied their fuel.

My uneasiness only grew when Steve Sitzman arrived with his equipment and began the earthmoving. Up to this point I had worked hard to bring the cropped-out fields back to health, adding lime and manure, and reseeding them to pasture grasses and legumes. When Steve dropped the blade of his behemoth bulldozer and began peeling away huge swaths of topsoil, however, I saw with a sickening feeling how all of that patient, healing work — mine for a few years, and nature's for millennia — could be undone and destroyed in a manner of days or even hours.

Steve's skills are legendary in this area, however, and as I watched him work, I found my discomfort fading, replaced by sheer fascination and admiration. He was careful not to mix the various soil layers, so they could be put back in the right place. Merely by eyeballing, he got the basement hole dug to within inches of spec, then finished with a transit level and got it perfect. He dug the pond right, with a keyway dam and packed clay where it belonged, guaranteeing it would not leak or give way. He wasted no motion, steering his track hoe into a new position even as he simultaneously swung it around and deftly repositioned its huge hydraulic arm and bucket. It was, in a way, like watching a ballet performance, albeit with a 40,000-pound dancer. Through it all, I got the strange sense that somehow, even with his massively powerful and potentially destructive equipment, Steve was being *gentle*. True, he was changing the landscape irreversibly. But as I thought of the fish and frogs and fowl that would come to occupy the pond and the family that would occupy a house rising out of that basement hole, I said a hopeful prayer that the changes were, finally, for the better.

We broke ground in June and were expecting in September, so I spent a busy summer making as much progress as possible. Paul's daughter and son-in-law had decided to build about the same time; throughout the summer we gathered crews that worked one day on their place and the next on ours. At one of these work-a-thons, we poured the concrete foundation footers and set the first courses of Lego-like Styrofoam blocks that would become the insulating forms for the poured basement walls. After everyone left, I discovered that one of my crew members had set a block improperly, making the foundation slightly out of square and creating a problem that would carry its way up through the rest of the house. Though the mistake was minor, I threw my first (but far from my last) honest-to-goodness house-building tantrum, warming up some four-letter words on which I would put a lot of mileage over the next few years. Building the barn had been one thing, but this was something altogether different for my perfectionist tendencies to deal with. They would end up fighting tooth and nail the idea that the building process would require reconciling oneself to such errors, especially insofar as it depended on the help of others less exacting than I was. Cyndi reminded me again and again that the building process and the relationships that surrounded it were more important than the perfection of the product, but it was a hard, hard lesson to learn.

Mistakes and frustrations aside, however, it was a glorious summer. Every day brought visible progress, camaraderie among the work crews, and memorable stories to last a lifetime. Once the basement walls and floor were poured, we began the framing. Although I had romantic ideas about building with used lumber from old barns and houses, I soon realized that I lacked the time, patience, and resourcefulness to hunt it down and reclaim it, and so had a local building supply company deliver two truckloads of dimensional lumber and sheet goods. As the materials slid off the trucks and I prayed forgiveness for whatever Canadian forest had suffered to supply them, I also thrilled to think that those bundles would somehow become the shell of our home.

Slowly, the house grew up like the trees from which it was made. In a lovely full circle, I called Scott Sanders, my old English professor with whom I had stayed in touch and who had helped inspire much of the life I had chosen, and he came down from Bloomington with his wife, Ruth, to help me install the four-by-eight sheets of subflooring for the main level. As Cyndi and Ruth visited in the apartment and kept us hydrated and fed, Scott and I nailed down sheet after sheet, in one breath relaying measurements or grunting with effort, in the next reflecting together on Emerson and Thoreau—a rare synthesis in which we both felt wonderfully whole. By the end of that long but much-too-short day, we had renewed our friendship, enjoyed good conversation, and finished with the subfloor, to boot. Ruth, Cyndi, Scott, and I gazed at the expansive platform of unbroken flooring and agreed that going on to frame the upstairs would only ruin a great place to dance.

Continue we did, however, for the summer dwindled and Cyndi's due date neared. I knew we would not have the house livable by the time the baby came, but I hoped not to live as a trio for too many months in the ever-smaller apartment. So as Cyndi sweltered bravely without air conditioning through her third trimester, I worked alone and with groups of friends to frame the upstairs. We affixed a long gin pole on the loader bucket of Paul's farm tractor and used it to set the roof trusses in place. The ease and speed with which we did so was a happy contrast to the stumbling barn-raising experience, and I realized that while no expert carpenter, I was at least no longer a novice. The sense of agency and competence I felt, however misplaced it may have been, gave me a confidence and satisfaction that I rarely experienced in either my studies or my white-collar professional work. I was doing something wonderfully real and tangible, something almost archetypally right: I was building shelter for my family, which would always stand (I hoped) as a sacrament of my love for them and for this place.

Once a subfloor is down, the walls and roof must follow very, very soon so as to keep rain from rotting it. A professional framing crew can accomplish this in a few days or a week, but with only my own and occasional volunteer and hired labor, the pace was much slower. When Cyndi went into labor a week early in September, the house was fully formed but skeletal, and certainly far from being "in the dry." I had hoped to be much farther along in the construction when Cyndi gave birth, but when are we ever truly prepared for major changes?

Cyndi's labor was long and hard, and when it didn't progress as it should, she had an emergency ultrasound, which up to that point our crunchy granola, *au-naturale* prenatal care decisions had led us to spurn. The technician discovered the problem: the baby was situated in a transverse-breech position, stalling the labor. She also discovered another surprise: unbeknownst to us or our doctor, Cyndi was carrying twins! So in yet another irony (I was beginning to get used to them), rather than the unanesthetized, doula-assisted natural birth for which we had hoped and prepared, Cyndi had an emergency C-section, and she delivered blessedly healthy, identical twin girls: Eva, whose name we had agreed upon if we had a girl, and Clare, whose name occurred to both of us simultaneously in the operating room.

In the days that followed, as Cyndi recovered from the physical and emotional trauma of the surgery, we did our best to adjust to the idea of having unexpected twins. I tried in vain not to fret about the fact that it rained on the exposed subfloor for the entire week we were in the hospital. Many friends were generous with gifts and support, but even so, both of us were utterly overwhelmed. Having a child in the midst of this house-building venture was difficult enough to contemplate, but having two almost snapped the spine of our resolve.

The day we were to leave the hospital, I struggled to strap the two infant seats into Cyndi's very small car. In the fog of my exhaustion and anxiety, I somehow tangled and jammed the seatbelt mechanism, and as the nurse was busy wheeling Cyndi and our babies down to meet me, I sat weeping in the back seat, utterly beaten before parenthood had even begun.

Mercy and momentum move us forward, however, so after a brief stay with my parents in Evansville, we made our bleary-eyed way back to the farm to start our new life as a family of four. We threw out any "extraneous" furniture (like our couch, chairs, and end tables) to make room in the small apartment for a crib and the copious equipment and supplies that infants seemed to require.

Some of the most invaluable help we received came from unexpected sources. The wife of a Saint Meinrad colleague—herself a mother of seven, including two sets of twins!—coordinated a food brigade, relieving us from cooking for several weeks. A kindly, late-middle-aged student at Saint Meinrad, a long-distance grandmother of twins, took it upon herself to visit often, doing some vicarious grandparenting and giving Cyndi a break from childcare. All this help left us with contradictory feelings of gratitude and abandonment. We were thankful for the wonderful favors from so many, and yet we also came to see how occasional the help was, relative to the 24/7 schedule parenting demands.

Though proximity to my mother and stepfather had been a driving force of my settling back in southern Indiana, they were still some distance away, and their lives were busy and full. An hour's drive ended up being a greater distance than we realized, and we saw far less of them than we had hoped. While we may have felt we needed a village to help raise these children, we realized that we didn't have one. The vast majority of the time, we were on our own to do the best we could. It was in many ways a bitterly disappointing thought and a cause of some resentment, but it gave us a strange sense of solidarity with most other parents in the country, who likewise struggle for support in raising their children. It also clarified our task, trimmed our expectations, and helped us move forward into the challenging gift of parenthood.

It is difficult to recollect and write about the months that followed, for though I rejoiced in our children, their birth marked my downward slide into a deep, dark season of depression and struggle for both Cyndi and me. We had foreseen how much this period would demand of us and had tried our best to rest up and prepare for it before the house-building began in earnest. Any challenge for which one can adequately prepare, however, is really no great challenge at all. This experience was indeed a great challenge, and having been able to stockpile only so much energy, our reserves were rapidly running out.

In a marathon weekend of work, Paul brought his family with him, and together we got the roof sheathing and tar paper installed. Within a few days I had nailed on all of the four-by-eight sheets of blueboard insulation onto the wall framing, and at last, the house was fully formed and in the dry. Though this was a major accomplishment—not to mention a great relief—it also signaled the end of a period in which each day would show obvious and visible progress in the shape of the house. I turned to the tedious tasks of wiring and plumbing. Cyndi's parents came out from Pennsylvania, staying for a few days and sleeping in a camping trailer we borrowed. Cyndi's mom provided her a brief reprieve from the suffocating isolation of stay-at-home mothering, while her dad, who likewise had built his family's house thirty years earlier, helped me begin the wiring. The visit arrived like the Christ-child: a much-needed light in a time of darkness.

Jesus' birth may have brought light into the world, but it took a while, and the brunt of winter still followed that night of nights in Bethlehem. Likewise, I plunged deeper into darkness as day after day I pulled wire and soldered pipes. I tried my best to remain present to Cyndi, Eva, and Clare, but to be honest, for several months I saw little of the three most important people in my life, and my thoughts were almost fully occupied by various practical problems to be solved. I had heard horror stories of how house-building projects had destroyed marriages and broken up families, and feeling the strain in our own relationship, I realized that we were not immune to such dangers. Cyndi and I had many difficult conversations in which we both wondered if we and our marriage could survive this project. I felt a constant tension: my love for my family had moved me to create a home for them, but creating that home pulled me away, in mind and body, from the ones I loved. The time when Cyndi felt the most overwhelmed and most needed my help was precisely the period in which I could least offer it.

We tried our best to support each other with the few resources we had, but in many ways, we both felt abandoned.

In retrospect, our main survival mechanism was emotional anesthesia: our mutual willingness to go numb for a while. Though Cyndi and I prayed briefly together each evening, a habit that has been salvific to our marriage, beyond that my own prayer life was a shambles. Most days, the best I managed was a half-hearted offering of my work to God. I felt thoroughly disconnected from all things divine: not so much that God had abandoned me, but that I had abandoned God, my myopic focus on building having excluded almost every other spiritual or emotional sensitivity.

I slept little and poorly, staying up late to work and awakened often, either by our twins' nighttime feeding schedule, my anxiety about various vexing construction issues, or both. Though I normally began working on the house at 4:30 or 5:00 in the morning, many nights I strapped on a tool belt at 2:00 or 3:00 a.m., having given up the fruitless struggle to sleep.

My darkest hour came one such early morning in February. It was five degrees in the unheated shell of the house as I worked by battery-powered headlamp down in the dark basement, my feet blocks of ice; my ungloved, unfeeling fingers fumbling to measure, cut, and solder copper pipe. The crews of friends and neighbors, so essential during the glory days of rough construction, had long since turned to their own affairs, and I faced the work alone. I sat down on an overturned five-gallon bucket, rocking back and forth in a near-catatonic struggle to remember even one good reason why I had taken on this gargantuan, impossible project, for which all of us were paying so dearly. My prayer was a simple and desperate cry for divine help.

For those who excel by hiding their own fears and vulnerability behind a veil of competence and control, grace can often be found only after falling to the deep, dark bottom of the well. This was exactly where I felt myself to be, and I did not particularly like the person I discovered down in the well. I noted how prone I was to depression, anger, and resentment; how little patience I had with myself or others; how much I and those close to me suffered from my single-minded drivenness and perfectionism. A profound insight of the Christian tradition, however, is that the Paschal mystery lies at the heart of any real conversion or passage into maturity. You rise only by falling; you live only by dying; you grow upward to the heights only after tunneling or falling down into the depths, where you are forced to confront the stark realities of yourself and the world, shadows and all.

There in the depths, I had to let go of any notions that I was in control of my own life or anyone else's, or that by my own power I could overcome internal and external forces of destruction, disorder, darkness, and death. In this painful, naked awareness I realized that this place of brokenness is exactly where God can meet us most truly—not as an action-hero savior, but as a gentle, reassuring presence who, as the cross reveals, understands darkness from firsthand experience. Meeting us there in the depths, God does not clear away all the obstacles or dispel all the shadows but walks with us step by step toward true healing, authenticity, and growth.

Even so, I cannot say that I felt better after hitting bottom, that I experienced some definite turning point or sensed some divine hand lifting me gently out of the miry clay. Things continued to be hard for a long time. But slowly, almost imperceptibly at first, they got better. Dawn is a gradual process: it is hard to pinpoint exactly when night ends and day begins. Grace gave Cyndi and me the gift of continued survival and forward motion as we plodded along through our respective tasks and tried again and again to want what we had chosen. Grace carried our strained relationship; for while our marriage did not necessarily thrive during this period, neither did it break. Neglecting each other sometimes engenders a "creeping separateness" that can destroy a marriage, and we were fortunate to learn this without going over the edge. I know all too well that it could have turned out very differently.

By grace, my body held up to overwork and under-rest. I suppose I could claim a certain amount of toughness; I got to know "Ole Willy," or long-term willpower and physical endurance. In truth, though, day after day of hard manual labor and little sleep quickly gave the lie to whatever illusions I may have harbored about my strength and stamina. Even a young, relatively fit and able body has its limits, and I found mine in fatigue, illness, and injury. When I fell two stories off the roof, the few split seconds of my plunge gave me a lot of time to think about how fragile a body is and how quickly it can be put out of commission. I was fortunate to walk (or rather, to limp) away from that mishap with only sore joints and a few cracked ribs, but I have not forgotten the object lesson: every one of us is breakable.

The wheel of the seasons gradually turned winter into spring, and little by little, I finished up the wiring, plumbing, insulation, and other tasks. As Eva and Clare neared their first birthday, hanging drywall became the next big project: hiding the complex spaghetti of wires and pipes behind smoothly finished walls. As I got ready for it, Cyndi remarked, "I never thought about how much *stuff* there is behind the walls!" I laughed, but we both realized how true her observation was, not only about house-building, but about people in general. We all have a lot of "stuff" hidden behind the façade we present to the world. Building had forced me to delve into the stuff of wiring and plumbing, but also the stuff of my own interior darkness and struggles. It was there, in that confusing maze, that God stayed with me and nudged me along.

I intended to hang the sheetrock myself, but having learned from the apartment that I found finishing drywall slow, difficult, and loathsome work, I hired Roger Goodley and his crew to do the taping, mudding, and sanding. Hailing from across the river in Owensboro, Kentucky, Roger was an amiable, self-effacing man in his mid-fifties, built like a linebacker, who wore wide red suspenders and loved to talk mainly about two things: how he was getting too old for drywall work, and Jesus.

"Whoo-ee, them ceilings is hard on a body! I oughta give it up," he would groan with a good-natured southern drawl, leaning back slightly while massaging his lower back with both hands, for added effect. "Problem is, I don't know how to do anything else, and I'm too old and dumb to start somethin' new."

When he bid the job, Roger told me he could either start a few days later or else in several months. In a panic about how to hang more than 10,000 square feet of drywall in such a short period of time, I took some emergency leave from Saint Meinrad and called on Cyndi and every other able-bodied person I knew, begging for help. Kyle Jackson, Paul's son-in-law with whom I had been trading work, helped move the mountainous stacks of sheetrock from the driveway, where the delivery driver had offloaded them sheet by sheet into the garage. My dad came out — as a "grunt," he claimed, in a strange reversal of father and son roles, not to mention a marked contrast to his job as a CEO of a healthcare corporation. As with the barn raising, our common work was the language of our love. Several others of the barn-raising crew returned for another stint of service. I took anyone and everyone who was willing, and worked them to the bone. Hanging drywall is hard on a body, too. Lugging fifty- and one-hundred-pound sheets through the house, hoisting them up and holding them in place, and then screwing them onto walls and ceilings—all of it made my helpers and me sore in places we didn't even know we had.

Over the course of seven straight sixteen-hour days, I worked harder than I knew I could, and then even harder when Roger Goodley and his crew came days earlier than expected and began mudding the upper floor while various helpers and I hurried to hang the basement sheetrock. Roger's men worked at a breakneck pace, even when one of them, an eighty-three-year-old finisher named Chester, took a few days off for cataract surgery—not because he had trouble mudding screw holes, which he claimed he could do blind, but because his cloudy vision was impeding his squirrel hunting. Roger drove them on, praising the Lord and complaining about his sore back. Soon, the evidence of all of those dark, torturous months' work at wiring and plumbing was hidden behind smoothly finished walls, ready for paint.

I hate painting. Cyndi and I had long agreed that if I would build the house, she would paint it. She invited several of her Louisville friends to help, and although they laughed, carried on meaningful conversation, and generally had a good time of it, the going was very slow.

As Cyndi's painting project was underway, I hired Kabe Beckman, a union millwright who was often laid off, to lay up creekstone on the exposed basement walls. In his spare time, Kabe and his family collected pieces of sandstone from various wooded areas around southern Indiana, hauled them to our place in an old dump truck, and painstakingly pieced and mortared them together in a huge, vertical jigsaw puzzle. More an artist than a tradesman in this regard, he did beautiful but slow work, and soon it became clear to him and to me that he had taken on a project far more than he could easily manage and on which he had bid far too low.

Kabe soldiered on, however, working quietly and steadily outside all summer as Cyndi struggled with the equally slow task of getting a primer coat and two coats of paint on a huge amount of sheetrock. Kabe took pity on her and offered to lend us his professional paint sprayer, with which I was able to complete the entire painting job in a two-day weekend marathon of spraying—thus making Cyndi both grateful and infuriated at once. The stonework and painting were finished at about the same time, and to celebrate, Kabe, Cyndi, and I feasted on Cyndi's homemade blackberry cobbler. Although we were squeezing blood out of every penny, we wanted to do right by someone who had done so right by us, and we wrote him a check for more than his bid.

Much, much work remained to be done, but almost a year after Eva and Clare were born, we were on the downhill slope. I graded the yard, using our farm tractor to redistribute the huge mountain of topsoil Steve Sitzman had so carefully piled up, and planted grass. We bought hickory flooring from a local sawmill run by two sisters, and I spent weeks cutting, fitting, and nailing it down on the entire main floor. Cyndi's parents came out again from Pennsylvania to help for a few days, staying once more in the small, borrowed camping trailer. Between good-natured complaints about his own bad back and knees, my father-in-law, a retired nuclear physicist who smashed atoms for fun, marveled jealously at the pneumatic nailer and other labor-saving tools of which he had been deprived when building three decades earlier.

In early fall, a year and a half into construction and six months later than my laughably optimistic plans, we decided to move in—despite the common wisdom of owner-builders that moving into an unfinished home practically guarantees that it will never be completed. In our case, however, we were so desperate to escape the confines of the barn apartment that we moved in with dozens of projects remaining, which gave us plenty of motivation to keep working. Reminiscent of my early days in the barn apartment, we had no front porch, deck, kitchen cabinets or counters, bathroom sink, interior doors, baseboards, or trim of any kind. I would spend the next several years on lovely but painstaking final touches, such as handmade maple cabinetry and a butcher-block island, solid wood doors, cherry trim I milled myself, and stone tile—even as our children soon got busy writing on the walls, crashing into things with tricycles, and otherwise making our yet-unfinished house look excessively lived in. On advice from my father-in-law, I'll call it done when I spend more time fixing what the kids destroy than completing the last few unfinished projects. By that measure, I'm getting pretty close.

Back when I first dreamed of house-building, I considered it a noble undertaking that would build character and virtue: a profound rite of passage by which I would prove myself "a man," worthy of the life I had chosen. Looking back, however, I have come to see how much it, like almost any significant undertaking, abounded with ambiguity. I accomplished more than anyone could have reasonably expected, but I also became very intimate with my physical limitations and, more importantly, my interior darkness: hot temper, depression, even despair. The merciful God I had come to know at Holy Comforter, who loves us beyond the categories of accomplishment or failure, often seemed hidden amidst the unrelenting pressure I put on myself to get things done and get them done right. By the time I got a fleeting glimpse of that God down in the dark frigid basement, I had finally realized how much I needed that God's loving, healing, redeeming presence in my life. We all do. The only question is the degree to which we are aware of our need and invite God to meet us in it.

Beyond the roller coaster of my emotional and spiritual journey, house-building gave me immeasurable practical knowledge and experience, which has helped me have more confidence about diving into other challenging projects, such as tractor repairs or the endless number of furniture projects Cyndi confidently commissions me to build. Though this practical handiness is increasingly rare in the urban, white-collar world, I found it is actually still fairly commonplace among my rural neighbors, many of whom have also built their own homes and think it thoroughly unremarkable that I did the same. I sometimes worry that both our economy and our culture have encouraged and even forced many people to become overspecialized to the point of making them almost helpless outside a narrow range of competence. I'm proud to have acquired some skill in various manual trades, but I also know I am a master at none of them. I have gained a profound respect for those who are truly artisans at their craft, like the earthmover Steve Sitzman, whose long years in the same trade gave his work an ease and grace that I know I may never achieve in any of mine.

Though I am far from an accomplished craftsman, house-building has nonetheless taught me the great satisfaction of creativity. I believe that being made in the image of an infinitely and incessantly creative God, and belonging in a world of unimaginable fecundity, human beings have embedded in our nature the desire to bring forth something new and beautiful — which, according to the Catholic sacramental imagination, reflects God's love at work in the world. I'm always mindful that building this house exacted great costs, both as a financial and a personal toll my family and me, as well as on the earth that provided both the raw materials and the energy required for its construction and maintenance. Even so, I look at our home as a tangible sacrament of my care for my family, of our commitment to this location, and of our desire to create a place of warmth and welcome for all we encounter. As all creative work should be, it is a kind of incarnation in which love takes on flesh—or rather, concrete, wood, drywall, and paint—and becomes a material reality: our particular *logos* being born into the world.

At the same time, because every worthwhile creative endeavor requires hard work and determined willpower to see it through to completion, and since this effort is often driven by ego as well as grace, I have found it tempting (whenever I conveniently forget the dark cloud of depression in whose shadow I did much of the building) to identify myself with this home as an extension or expression of myself. I want to say proudly, "I built that"—with emphasis on the *I*. But this "I" is the ego-self, which, as Thomas Merton has rightly observed, is not the deepest or truest self. So despite all I have invested in this house, I try always to remember that it is ultimately not a safe repository for my identity, since any *thing* I create can become an idol, a pile of ashes, or both. I don't make myself through what I make.

My truest self, I began to learn in that dark basement, is a gift from beyond: beyond the bounds of ego; beyond the small, cramped, sham self that exults in trophies of accomplishment and worries about their destruction. The real root of my identity is the image of God within me: a self made not just for creativity, but for communion—with the world, with others, and with God. The essence of both creativity and identity, then, is not in the tangible *things* that we make, much less the ego wrapped up in them, but in the connections forged in the making—connections that are the threads of true love. True creativity is an act of communion, which helps us live more fully into a life of belonging.

This side of heaven, however, belonging is never easy or complete. My Benedictine colleagues and the *Rule of Benedict* itself have taught me that real community is not a panacea, not a club or a clique, but a school of ongoing conversion and a place of unvarnished truth. Building our house helped me relate more deeply to my neighbors, my friends, and my family, and this deeper connection has shown me how all of us are by turns generous and apathetic, easy-going and uptight, conscientious and careless, gentle and unkind. A life of true connection with others fits us for the divine life: both when we cooperate and rejoice together, and when tension and conflict reveal our great need for mercy and (if we allow them) wear off our sharper edges so that we might offer and receive it. Though it felt excruciatingly lonely at times, building our house was a communal effort, and it helped me see how God saves us: *in* community, *by* community, and *for* community.

PART TWO

chapter five

Farming and Food

When Cyndi and I began to contemplate building a house, my uncle Ron gave me some advice. It was the only counsel I ever received from him that I did not fully heed. "Be careful about getting too deep into this building project," he warned me, "or you'll forget that farming is the reason you came out here in the first place." In many ways, Ron was right, and there were a couple of years in which our farm suffered neglect while I was busy being overwhelmed by the effort to get one or the other roof over our heads. But just as the Psalmist could not forget Jerusalem even in exile, farming has remained the star I followed to this place and that guides me through the vocational struggles I have had over the years.

I bought land and chose the life of a farmer with my head full of ideals about a healthier sort of agriculture, gleaned from a lot of reading and a little bit of experience. I recognize that eating is an act as powerful as it is unavoidable, with environmental, social, political, and personal consequences: what I put in my mouth every day inevitably dictates what I become and the kind of world I help create. Eating poorly brings disease and destruction to our own bodies, the human community, and the land itself. Eating wisely and well can be a sacred act of communion, a source of great pleasure and satisfaction as well as a means of profound healing for the Creation.

From the time I first cracked open Wendell Berry's *Unsettling of America* in college, it has become ever more clear to me how profoundly broken modern agriculture is, and how all of us who enjoy its benefits—cheap, plentiful food—are complicit in its failure. At first glance, the huge increases in crop yield and labor productivity delivered by industrial agriculture appear to be one of the great marvels of the modern world. But they have come at steep cost. Healthy topsoil is absolutely indispensible for growing food, but a third of American topsoil, which is essentially irreplaceable on any reasonable (i.e., human) time scale, has been eroded away by the careless farming of annual crops, such as the corn, wheat, and soybeans that surround my farm (much of which is fed to livestock that would be far healthier if raised on grass). The soil that remains is degraded by overuse of chemical fertilizers, herbicides, and pesticides, and compacted by ever-larger, all-wheel drive equipment that can operate on soft ground. More diverse (and hence more resilient) ecosystems are destroyed and replaced by large monocultures, and pollution from farm chemicals harms flora, fauna, and watersheds both near and far.

If farming were a lucrative business, all of this ecological destruction would be somewhat more understandable, at least in a cynical sort of way that assumed people were driven only by self-interest. But given the high costs of land, chemicals, fuel, and equipment, the vagaries of weather, and generally low prices for farm commodities (driven down by overproduction), the only way most American farmers profit or break even is by taxpayer-supported government welfare in the form of crop subsidies. And even with subsidies, many farmers—or rather, *former* farmers—still can no longer make a decent living from their acreage. Some who are stubborn (and fortunate, like I am) can find off-farm jobs that support their money-losing operations. If they cannot find work, they migrate from farms to urban areas where it can be found. In a vicious downward spiral, rural economies suffer, both because of declining populations and fewer local businesses that keep money circulating in the community. I have come to learn that in my county, for example, the small town of Newtonville used to have a sawmill, gristmill, cooper shop, brick kiln, wagon shop, blacksmith shop, undertaker, milliner's shop, hotel, barber shop, shoemaker, post office, two general stores, several restaurants, a garage, a trucking business, two churches, a saloon, an American Legion post, two doctors, and a school. All that remains of this once-thriving local economy is the grubby, cinder-block Legion building and a few houses. Almost every other small town in my county has a similar history and has suffered a similar decline; today, we all drive an hour to do most of our business.

With fewer people in rural areas and fewer businesses and services available for them, the rural social fabric frays and weakens. There are fewer civic organizations, community events, and support services. There is less opportunity for neighborly interaction and cooperation. Those who remain often seek unhealthy solace from loneliness and stress through television, obsessive web-surfing, or addiction to drugs and alcohol. Families are strained and often broken by isolation, financial hardship, or both.

Not only rural landscapes, economies, and communities suffer, however. Those who live in cities and suburbs, which is most of us, are also affected by changes brought about by modern agriculture. With so few employed or employable by industrial agriculture, cities and suburbs become densely packed and thus overbuilt, starving many — especially the urban poor — of any meaningful connection to healthy natural landscapes. The shift of population from country to city has often resulted in chronic unemployment or employment that is unhealthy, unfulfilling, and underpaid. Community life is plagued by the obvious problems of poverty, violence, and other crime, but also by the unhappiness of so many people who are bored, discontent, and isolated from each other and from Creation. Individual health suffers, both because of the rat race that often makes a healthy lifestyle impossible, and because while a motivated few with wealth and mobility might be able to frequent farmers' markets, the vast majority of urban and suburban dwellers rarely experience truly fresh, healthy food.

The problems of modern agriculture are daunting, but solutions are at hand as well, and there is a movement to bring health back to our land, our economic system, and our rural and urban communities. Wendell Berry, Michael Pollan, and others point the way to a more careful, more sustainable way of growing and eating food. Pollan's simple formula is a good basic guide: "Eat food. Not too much. Mostly plants."[1] In other words, we would forgo highly processed products and instead eat *real* food like vegetables and fruits and whole grains, far less meat (and this raised mainly on grass rather than grain), and fewer calories overall. Rather than eating food grown in the monoculture fields of this country or Brazil, Canada, or China and trucked or flown thousands of miles to our plates, we would adapt our diets toward foods our local area can produce and the seasons in which that food is available.

Instead of our food dollars and our taxes going to maintain large grain farms and the confinement livestock operations for which most of that grain is grown (if it's not being made into high-fructose corn syrup), we would support smaller-scale, more ecologically sensitive and labor-intensive farming. Poor and rich alike would buy less food in grocery stores and more at an increasing number of farmers' markets; some might buy shares in a community-supported agriculture farm, paying a farmer an upfront lump sum in exchange for a weekly supply of produce throughout the growing season. Whether in cities or in the country, those with even a little land for a garden might grow some of their own food.

Changing how and what we eat would, of course, require many more small farms than currently exist. This in turn would necessitate a "resettling" of America, in which migration patterns would reverse, and those in urban and suburban areas would begin to repopulate the countryside, taking up small-scale farming as a satisfying, healthy, and profitable livelihood or avocation, or starting businesses that support and contribute to a stronger rural economy. Such a shift toward decentralization and regional self-sufficiency could mitigate many of the economic and social ills of both country and city, as well as establish strong relationships between the two that are so necessary for the health of each.

In light of this hopeful though admittedly idealistic vision, I saw sustainable farming not only as a lifestyle I would enjoy, but as a vocation in which I could do my part to help save the world. After taking my leap of faith, however, I soon found myself grappling with the many challenges and disillusionments the life entailed. To begin, I quickly came to discover how utterly ignorant I was about farming. I had read extensively and even done real work on other farms, but facing the task of turning my newly purchased, overgrown fields into a profitable farm, I found myself as overwhelmed as I had been building my house.

Acquiring and repairing my collection of old, tired, but marginally functional farm machinery had been the least of my farming challenges (though that had been challenging enough). The land itself, I suspected and then confirmed through extensive soil testing, had been abused and exhausted by conventional farming. It was low in all the major nutrients, and while the bottomland near the creek had plenteous topsoil for this region—twenty-four to thirty inches deep in places—the topsoil on the hillier ground had eroded to less than a foot thick. Here I discovered a crucial difference between gardening and farming—a difference of scale. In a small garden, if you have little or poor soil, you can truck in topsoil and compost, add leaves and grass clippings and other organic matter, and quickly build up the fertility of your little plot. Even on a small farm, however, when the land in need of fertilization is measured in acres rather than square feet, it is much more of a challenge to obtain the tonnage required for real soil rejuvenation. And even if you could, it is a hard truth that this is simply stealing fertility from elsewhere.

I concentrated most of my efforts on the few acres of our market gardens, and even then, I initially hauled in and spread about half a million pounds of cow manure, and have been adding more ever since. The rest of the open ground I established as clover and fescue hay, spreading several tons of crushed lime and an occasional application of oh-so-fragrant hog manure from what is euphemistically called a "honey wagon," but otherwise I had to rely on nature's own slow but reliable power of self-healing.

Even aside from restoring the fertility of the cropland, I found market gardening to be a daunting challenge. Market gardening is essentially a scaled-up home garden. As opposed to conventional monocrop cash grain agriculture, which requires you to be an expert in just a few crops, market farming or extensive gardening generally entails growing dozens of diverse vegetable and fruit crops, each with its own special requirements for cultivation and harvest. I found myself awash in a sea of practical questions about farming. What are the fertility demands of potatoes? When do you start tomato seedlings? What is the proper row spacing for broccoli? What is the best crop to plant after cabbages? How, for crying out loud, can you tell when melons are ripe? Unlike rowcrop farming, which is entirely mechanized, market gardening also requires a great deal of physical labor. I do use a tractor and other mechanical implements for tillage, haymaking, manure spreading, and some weed cultivation, but even with that, there is no avoiding a lot of hard work: we do all of our planting, transplanting, weeding, and harvesting by hand.

Aside from the challenge of producing crops, as a small-acreage market grower I still have to figure out some creative way to sell them; I can't simply truck bushel upon bushel of corn, soybeans, or wheat to the local grain storage elevator. Many market gardeners have contracts with local restaurants, grocery stores, and other wholesalers. Some sell shares or subscriptions through a community-supported agriculture arrangement. I have always been attracted to this model, and yet I can't seem to get up nerve to take a large sum of money from customers upfront and then have the weekly responsibility of having something ready with which to fill their grocery sacks. I cringe at the thought of highly principled and good-natured customers forcing themselves to cheerfully accept twenty-five pounds' worth of turnips, or enough carrots to turn their eyes orange, simply because that is what is available. Or worse, I can imagine my guilt if, because of uncooperative weather, some unforeseen disease or predation, or my own failure as a farmer, I lacked enough produce to fill the sack each week.

We maintain an e-mail list of customers who regularly buy our produce and our free-range eggs, and every week or so I send an e-mail out to everyone on it, letting them know what is available and how much it costs. We don't move huge amounts of produce this way, but it works well in that we don't spend time harvesting extra produce that then goes to waste. One of the customers on our list is the kitchen of Saint Meinrad Archabbey. Aside from the obvious benefit of having a larger-scale wholesale customer, it is a tremendous satisfaction to know that I am helping feed the monks, students, and staff that gather around the mission of the monastery.

Then there are the weekly farmers' markets. An iconic image associated with organic and small-scale farming, these markets are becoming increasingly popular in urban areas and are spreading to many rural areas, as well, including my own. Over the years, my family and I have been vendors at several, and I confess to having a love-hate relationship with them. I love the idea of farmers' markets. I believe in them strongly as a subversive alternative to the large-scale food economy. I appreciate all the relationships they have helped our family cultivate with the wider community. In general, I have had a wonderful experience with them.

Farmers' markets are a real practical challenge to me as a grower, however. Ensuring the freshest produce for our Saturday morning markets generally means harvesting late into Friday night and waking earlier than Trappist monks to continue harvesting on Saturday morning. We spend the remainder of the morning transporting produce to market and trying our best to sell it. Without much established market for organic produce in our rural area, and with many people gardening themselves or getting free surplus from neighbors, we have dealt with many skeptical customers who were reluctant to pay more for my vegetables. Inevitably, we drive home with a lot of produce unsold.

Despite all of the challenges of farming, however, like most farmers I know, I simply cannot imagine not doing it: it is an almost irresistible calling. I have spent the last ten years learning not only the difficulties that small-scale farming entails, but also discovering what it means to have farming as a deeply satisfying, God-given vocation.

I have heard a story, perhaps apocryphal, about a famous pianist who was approached by an admiring fan after a concert. The breathless young woman exclaimed, "I would give my life to play like you!" "My dear," the pianist replied, "I have." Such single-minded devotion is, thank heaven, for the few geniuses and monomaniacs among us; most of us will always have the blessed and difficult privilege of negotiating among many good but competing priorities, which is a hallmark of any intentionally lived life. In working this out for myself, over the past several years I have come to accept a shift in the role I thought farming would play in my life.

I was right in discerning that farming was my vocation. Encouraged by too many follow-your-dream, self-help and career counseling books, however, I made the mistake of assuming that if something is truly your vocation, you should earn your living at it. And I also assumed, wrongly, that each person is called to one primary vocation. My own experience, confirmed by the stories of vocation I have heard from hundreds of students in the graduate ministry programs I direct at Saint Meinrad, has led me to regard vocation as a much richer and more fluid idea than I had first considered. Unlike the virtuoso pianist, most of us have not one vocation but many simultaneous ones, and over the course of a life, vocations come, go, and evolve.

My job at Saint Meinrad has kept the farm capitalized, but it has also meant that I, like most farmers in the area, have had to squeeze my farming into early mornings, late evenings, and long hours on the weekends—an invitation to workaholism, especially when for several years I was also busy with home-building. With some wistfulness, I often think back to my idealized vision of the simple farming life, with few material needs and plenty of time to nurture the body, soul, and mind. My original plan had been to wean myself from off-farm income and to make my living as a full-time farmer. Ten years later, it hasn't happened yet, and when or if it might, I still don't know.

This isn't simply because it's hard to make a living farming, although it is. Many clever farmers, such as Joel Salatin and Eliot Coleman, have nonetheless found a way to earn a good full-time income by providing healthy agricultural products. In my case, almost without my realizing it, my understanding about what it could mean to farm as a vocation gradually evolved. I began to see that the particular set of gifts and proclivities God had given me did not necessarily fit with those of a full-time farmer.

While I loved the actual growing, I had less patience with and interest in the business of selling and marketing produce, especially when it was such an uphill struggle in this area to do so. I crave financial stability and security, and, of course, farming entails great risk: farmers may have a reputation for being conservative and conventional, but anyone who gambles significant amounts of capital and labor against bankers, weather, and the markets has to have nerves of steel. I love to write and read and otherwise pursue some semblance of an intellectual life, and to cultivate these interests requires time away from fields and farmers' markets. Two years after beginning work at Saint Meinrad, I was promoted to the directorship of a vibrant and growing Catholic lay ministry formation program, and suddenly I found my work full of challenge, purpose, and reward: far more than simply a day job that stole time from farming but paid its bills. More importantly, as I married and had children, I saw that quality family relationships cannot be fit into the few small nooks and crannies of time that were left over from farming, a full-time job, and a few hours of sleep. My primary vocation was as a husband and father; everything else would have to fall in line behind these roles.

Because of both principle and pride, I have always recoiled from the idea of "hobby" farming, or worse yet, from the elitist term "gentleman farmer." I feel too passionately about food and the need for healthy agriculture to think of farming and gardening merely as pleasant diversions or ways to maintain the romantic ideal of "connection to nature" for those who can afford to keep it at arm's length. Frederick Buechner was right when he wrote that vocation is where your deep gladness and the world's great needs intersect, but I believe the gladness of which he wrote is far deeper than mere enjoyment. Plenty of early mornings I would rather roll over and sleep in than be out in the fields at first light; plenty of Saturday afternoons I'd rather be anywhere else but elbow-deep in grease and tractor innards. The "gladness" of vocation rests on a much more solid foundation than pleasure: it's more a sense of rightness, goodness, truth, and meaning. I love to farm, not only because most of the time I enjoy what I do as a farmer, but more profoundly, because I *believe* in the healing work that good farming is—both for the ailing earth and for my own woundedness.

If growing good food can be good work and a vocation *per se*, then it matters less if and how much I am paid to do so, if the scale of my operation is a farm or just one small raised bed, and if that vocation has to share pride of place with the vocations of family, friendship, the life of the mind, and the building up of the world in other ways. In fact, as I've thought through these questions, I've taken great comfort from Gene Logsdon, the author and "Contrary Farmer" from northern Ohio, who has long insisted that our broken agricultural system would make great strides toward health precisely if more Americans became small-scale "hobby farmers." He believes that those with an off-farm job or on-farm cottage industry to support their farming could farm small acreages well, rather than having to farm a lot of ground and cut a lot of corners simply to make ends meet if farming is a full-time livelihood.

Although I still contend with my pride, it has been tremendously liberating to realize that I don't need to be a large-scale, full-time farmer in order to be a "real" farmer. Freed from the inexorable burden of profit-making, I can worry less about the inefficiencies of time and capital and spend more time growing food as best I can and enjoying the process—at least on average, if not at every moment. I can begin, as Cyndi has wisely urged me, to see the growing of food as a ministry that serves our family, our customers, and the earth itself.

This has helped me see the farmers' markets in a new light, worrying less about what we're clearing that morning and more about the people we serve and the connections we make. At a recent market in a nearby town, I was parked two stalls over from a sweaty, scowling, nearly toothless old man who had come with his wife and grandson from the small town of Otwell to sell his garden produce. His dirty workpants rode low under his substantial belly, held up by both a belt and a pair of wide, black suspenders. A beat-up straw hat, with large holes worn through the brim, perched on his balding head. His old Chevy truck was piled high with sweet corn, and the bedrails were loaded with flats of tomatoes. His stick-thin wife looked like a nervous chain smoker on her first day of trying to quit cold turkey.

The old man's ten-year-old grandson had cruised around the market all morning in a black Harley Davidson t-shirt, playing with a stack of pennies, until he finally got bored with them and gave them to me. I thanked him for the pennies and gave him one of my watermelons. He hesitated to take it, so I told him, "OK, I've sold it to you for nine cents." His grandfather came over as we talked, and the grizzled old man spoke gruffly: "That boy ain't beggin' no watermelon off ya, is he?" I explained to him about his grandson's generous act of giving the pennies, and that I was just trying to respond in kind. He accepted this, albeit somewhat warily.

In John's Gospel, the feeding of the five thousand came about because one small boy proffered what appeared to be a pittance in the face of so much need: five barley loaves and two small fish. In this miracle, Jesus transformed a crowd into a community through that boy's seemingly inconsequential generosity. My simple exchange with Grant somehow worked a similar miracle in me. Even though nine pennies for a watermelon was the cheapest I'd ever sold one, in that moment my resentments about depressed produce prices and my abstract worries about agriculture fell away like scales from my eyes, and I understood, as Thomas Merton once did in downtown Louisville, that all of us in that market belonged to each other; that everyone was walking around, shining like the sun. I had gone to the market with the intention of feeding others; I left feeling fed myself and gave away the rest of my unsold melons to neighbors on the drive home.

The Pleasures of Food

Although I was drawn to farming because of my environmental convictions and my belief that as a vocation it fit well with my interests and my gifts, much of the draw was quite simple: my growing love of good food. I have never been a restaurant connoisseur or even a very good cook, but ever since a brief dating relationship with an aspiring chef in my last year of college, I have tried to make up for all of those years I wasted on meat, potatoes, and junk food. Good food is expensive, however, and I am cheap, so I think it is wonderful that living on a farm allows me to have produce fresher than any amount of money can buy. There is simply no way to replicate the taste of sweet corn, for example, that is picked and shucked with the water already boiling, thrown in the pot for a few minutes, and eaten right away with butter and salt.

As I have come to love good food more and more, I have realized a great irony of American eating: although we eat all the time and many of us are overweight, as a culture we actually seem to hate food—real food, at any rate, as Michael Pollan would define it. We eat highly processed products, which are not only stripped of their nutritive value and loaded with questionable and unpronounceable chemicals, but also just don't taste very good. Most of us eat out of sync with the seasons and our own bioregion. We often eat too much—not until we're sated, much less until we feel 80 percent full as recommended by the Japanese custom of *Hara hachi bu*, but until our large plates are empty and our stomachs are unpleasantly stuffed. We eat carelessly and quickly, grabbing a bite in the drive-through and eating it in the car, or munching through television programs. Increasingly, we eat alone: the family meal or dinner with friends has become a rare phenomenon and perhaps an endangered species.

Farming has spurred our family—as tough economic times have for many in our country—to kindle a love affair with simpler, fresher, cooked-at-home meals. One of the anchors of our home economy has been our commitment to eat a good supper together almost every night. I am the chief grower and (at best) a sous chef; Cyndi has put her creative talents to work discovering and inventing recipes to make use of the produce I dump by the bucketload on our kitchen island all spring, summer, and fall, and from the freezer and pantry and root cellar we work hard to stock. Our children can be picky eaters at times, but it is easier to get them to eat their vegetables because they know that Papa raised them or they themselves helped. For the most part, as a family we simply enjoy food and the good company that good food has a knack for gathering.

Food as Sacrament

I don't think it was an accident that my interest in farming and food tended to parallel my attraction toward the Anglican and Catholic strains of Christianity. In these traditions, the central symbolic act of worship is the Eucharist, which draws, transforms, and binds together believers of every stripe in a common act of breaking bread and sharing wine. Eating is an inescapable and fundamental way in which we relate to the world, which Jesus, in centering so much of his ministry around meals, must surely have recognized. Like a sacrament, food is an outward and visible sign of a deeper, complex, and generally hidden reality. It can be a symbol of destruction, as when poorly grown food represents the layers of personal, cultural, economic, political, and environmental ill health that are its causes or effects. It can be a symbol of health and healing, as when a simple, delicious, and nutritious meal embodies the love and care involved in its growing, sharing, and eating. Like the Eucharist, good food represents the partnership between human and divine effort: fruit of the earth, whose seasons and cycles of growth are in God's control; and the work of human hands, which cooperate with nature and nature's God to coax crops from the soil.

As our family has become more intentional about our meals, I've come to see that eating good food also follows a pattern of communion and mission, which is the core of Christian discipleship. In my parish, as at countless others, we gather together every week to be fed: by the Word of God and at the Eucharistic table. These liturgical acts of remembrance, reconciliation, and renewal embody rich, complex layers of symbol and tradition. But beyond all of this, they are also the immediate, tangible reality of bread on the tongue and wine in the gullet: a common meal shared with my fellow parishioners amid the sound of screaming children and imperfectly sung hymns. At this "source and summit" of faith, we are gathered together and fed, and then sent out, in the strength of that food and fellowship, on a mission: "to love and serve the Lord," whether by spreading the light of the Gospel to those seeking faith or simply living as a faithful disciple in all things great and small.

When we eat well at home, we echo this pattern. Any healthy food comes from the communion of sunlight, water, soil nutrients, and the rich genetic history of the seed, wedded with the knowledge, skill, and patience of the grower. We gather the harvest from field or farmer or market, and the various ingredients come together in the kitchen, transformed into something new. When food is on the table, the promise of pleasure and nourishment draws my family (and often our friends) back into community. Even those who eat alone are not truly alone, for if modern particle physicists are correct, in eating we commune with the entire universe. The atoms in our meal are billions of years old; many came from distant stars; and a few once belonged to the body of Jesus himself. In digesting we incorporate into our body's fibers the mind-bending reaches of time and space. When we eat, we are in solidarity with all that brought our meal to our plates—which is, ultimately, the entire history of the universe.

I aspire to a home economy that would recognize meals as acts of deep communion. Instead of the rote meal prayers my family and I often say, I aspire to utter a truly mindful meal prayer, which would remember and celebrate these far-reaching connections. It would acknowledge that wherever love is, God is, and that food grown, prepared, and eaten with love has a special sacredness. I would like to pray and eat with knowledge and intention so that the meal draws us closer to all who made the meal possible, to the Creation from which it came, to those with whom we break bread, and to the Creator from whose hands all good things come.

As with the Eucharistic liturgy, eating as an act of true communion will always lead to mission. A large part of this mission is and should be circular: we come to the table to be fed so that we may grow, purchase wisely, and prepare another meal for that same table, to be fed again. But just as St. Paul broke open the closed, circular logic of the Corinthians' slogan, "Food is meant for the stomach and the stomach for food," by placing eating within a larger context of discipleship, the faithful home economy is not an inward-focused, isolated life of simplicity and subsistence, but an outward-looking one of service. Certainly, the world will not heal until we learn to practice the arts of gentle and sustainable living, of putting our own houses in order. But even if everyone had "five acres and independence," as the classic homesteading book by that title recommends, and we all minded our own business, ours would be a sad and lonely world.

There will always be some who, because of unwise choices, the accident of birth and circumstance, or simply illness, old age, and infirmity (and who escapes these?), will lack the ability to provide for themselves. As Jesus said, we will always have the poor among us. And at some point, all of us will become poor in this sense: we will have to set down the axe, hoe, and kitchen knife to let others take care of us, just as we also required when we were infants and children.

Even if we are strong and able, most of us depend on the knowledge, labor, resources, and community of other people. Unless we have primitive needs, ingenious resourcefulness, and exceptional health, our home economies will always be linked with each other in mutual responsibility and service. This is, I believe, as it should be. In the interconnected and interdependent world God has created and sustains, we are made to need each other—and so we are made to serve each other. A healthy marriage is one in which one partner serves the other and vice-versa; the healthy congregation is one in which the pastor serves the parish and vice versa; the healthy home economy is one that serves and is served by the surrounding community and the world at large. Loving service is the core of mission, and I think it is also the meaning of true belonging. We may and we must love and serve our neighbors, both those near-at-hand and those in distant places or distant generations who are affected by our choices. This service-oriented love is an invitation to lose ourselves—at least our selfish, false, ego-oriented selves—and find our true selves again in God, whose image is imprinted on those around us and on the tapestry of Creation itself. Through such love, human community and the entire Creation could not only heal, but blossom.

chapter six

Children at Play

My mother and stepfather keep a wonderful picture on their refrigerator. Taken just a few days after Cyndi and I returned back to our farm from the hospital with Eva and Clare, the shot features Cyndi and me, each with a baby in our arms, standing in what will be the kitchen of our under-construction house. I'm wearing work clothes and a tool belt, and in the background of the photo, the fields, woods, and blue sky are visible through the house's as-yet unroofed, unwalled skeleton. Though they are surrounded by the gargantuan project of the unfinished house, beyond which lies an expansive swath of Creation, our tiny, helpless little children nonetheless command the entire focus of the photo.

That photo speaks volumes about how I felt as a new father. Despite my best efforts to prepare myself for fatherhood, the truth was that I was thoroughly unready. I was unprepared for the surprise of twins in the middle of house-building, of course, as well as the relentlessness of diapers and late-night feedings. Most of all, I was caught off guard by the tremendous sense of responsibility I felt for them. Through the mystery of love and biology, Cyndi and I had brought two new human beings into the world, and to love them meant, among many other things, to provide a true home for them. A bricks-and-mortar home, of course, which stood radically unfinished just sixty feet from our crowded barn apartment, but even more importantly, a home in the world at large. I had held strong environmental and social justice convictions for years, but having children brought those abstract principles into real and tangible focus. Now I wanted a better world not only for anonymous people in other places and generations, but also as a fitting inheritance and habitation for our own precious daughters.

For the first year or so of Eva's and Clare's lives, with me busy trying to get a roof over their heads, Cyndi was the primary eyewitness to all their early developmental milestones, and she was the one who noticed the subtleties of their different personalities and proclivities. Once most of the urgent house building work was behind me, however, I was able to pay more attention. I began to see them not just as helpless little creatures requiring constant care, but as two unique souls (though identical twins, our girls were differently tempered from day one) whom we had the privilege and challenge of rearing into adulthood. Like fatherhood as a whole, this responsibility grew gradually larger in my psyche until its magnitude dwarfed all others, especially when, three and a half years after our twins were born, we welcomed our third child, Elijah, for whose gestation, birth, and early months I was much more present.

As we contemplated getting married, Cyndi and I often discussed a core set of convictions about how we wanted to raise our children. Though like any parents we wanted them to be smart, capable, independent, and successful, most of all we wanted to raise them to be lovers: of themselves, others, Creation, and God. With climate change, overpopulation, degraded ecosystems, and various other social and political woes, our children will inherit a world rife with great challenges, much in need of people with deep stores of gentleness, kindness, and compassion. It will be a world requiring healing and justice. It will be a leaner world, where by choice or necessity, more people will do with fewer luxuries so that all may have a chance at survival. It will be, finally, a world where creativity must be nurtured. Creative people will add to the world's beauty—and as Dostoevsky rightly observed, the world will be saved by beauty. Creative people will be needed to discover and craft new ways of walking lightly and using limited resources with care and restraint.

I have long thought that love is as love does. So from my perspective, part of teaching our children to love has meant trying to empower them with practical knowledge and skills, which our life on a small working farm requires, and which will serve them well in whatever kind of life they end up leading amidst the challenges ahead. I want them to learn the manifold arts of healthy home economics, from fixing meals to fixing equipment, and to see the tangible, satisfying connections between the work they do and their basic needs being met. This tutelage began at a very early age. Often I would be pulling weeds or harvesting plants with a child in a backpack carrier, and a few times I even sandwiched myself between Eva in a front carrier and Clare in a backpack carrier, carrying them as I guided the tiller back and forth and cultivated the long crop rows.

Once they could walk, our children tagged along with Cyndi and me in the regular round of chores our home economy requires. For the most part they have played alongside us as we worked; mimicked me with hopeful clumsiness and toy versions of my tools; and with heartbreaking sweetness, "helped" in ways that generally cause a project to take more time rather than less. As they get older, however, Eva and Clare have begun to take on real responsibilities, mothering their little brother, helping to clean the house and wash the dishes, and daily gathering eggs from our flock of laying hens.

As with farm families time immemorial, I look forward to those few brief years when our kids can share more fully in our many tasks and chores. I want them to love the place as much as I do, but I also try to be realistic. I know that many of the people who grew up on a farm found the work so hard and the life so constricting that they were eager to leave as soon as they were of age, with little desire ever to return. Though I know how slim the odds are, nothing would please me more than that our kids avoid the temptation to flee in search of some chimerical "better" life, and instead stay or return, of their own volition, and take up the good work of caring intimately for the earth in a place where they have family and a history. So while I want them to know the meaning of hard work and real responsibility, I fear driving them as hard as I drive myself and driving them away from the life we have crafted largely for their sake.

How does one teach children to embrace work without breeding workaholism and resentment? A practice of Sabbath would be the antidote to a tendency toward the stereotypical "Protestant work ethic," in which rest is merely a means to enable more work. Far from teaching Sabbath to our kids, however, I have largely learned it from them, and from Cyndi, who shares neither my ambition nor my physical stamina. Family life has been my salvation in this regard, helping me let go of my need always to be *doing* something. Embracing Sabbath, even as imperfectly as I do, means recognizing the limits of our control, cultivating gratitude, and balancing work with rest, play, and wonder.

As long as I don't work them too hard, our kids naturally and instinctively explore the world, which is the only way for them to discover their deep and abiding connection to it. With an intimate familiarity with their particular place, their sense of belonging is rooted more in affection than any sort of abstract moral principle. In his fine book, *Last Child in the Woods*, Richard Louv argues that many of today's children suffer from "nature-deficit disorder" because modern American culture and parenting do not nurture meaningful relationships between children and the natural world. One of the saddest parts of this neglect is that introducing children to nature is so simple. It doesn't require trips to Yosemite or the Boundary Waters or any other wild places, though such trips are marvelous. It doesn't require living on a farm, though in such a life contact with the natural world is unavoidable. The only necessary thing for giving kids a profound experience of the natural world is to give them time, set them loose—in a park, in a woods, in a field, in a vacant lot, by a pond—and then let their inborn curiosity run its course.

This was a revelation to me and yet another discovery that our children were, of course, as much our teachers as our pupils. I had once imagined our kids to be a sort of tabula rasa on which we would do our best to inscribe our love and knowledge of the natural world. But this sort of top-down intentional instruction ended up being ancillary to their most authentic way of engaging the world. I believe that unless kids have their instincts thwarted by lack of opportunity or encouragement, they are hard-wired to explore and ask questions about their surroundings. We have had little need of lecturing our children; it is much more often the case that we are scrambling to keep up with their incessant barrage of questions: Why do trees lose their leaves? What is that chirping sound by the pond? How do chickens make eggs every day? Or my personal favorite: Why is water wet? Each of these questions, asked and engaged, creates one more tie that binds them to the world around them.

As important as curiosity are its handmaidens, wonder and imagination. Too often, I walk through our woodlot as an overly serious, pragmatic adult and see only board-feet of lumber or cords of firewood, or through a field of tall grass and see only a hay crop needing to be cut, raked, and baled. For our children, however, these same places are full of enchantment and adventure. I am often astounded to discover that our children have spent hours at a stretch playing make-believe in a fort they have discovered in the woods or made by trampling down a patch of uncut hay. Like the poet William Blake, they can spy angels perching in the branches of trees. Every crayfish hole is a "fairy hole" leading down to an exciting underground world of crystal caverns, lakes, and all manner of mysterious creatures. At their insistence, many of the bedtime stories I make up for them have their locus on the farm, which in the stories is full of "thin places" where something magical and mysterious awaits just behind the next tree.

I'm beginning to suspect that our children's imaginative vision of our farm is actually more helpful, healing, and ultimately more true than my much more practical way of seeing it. Good stewardship certainly demands tangible action guided by practical knowledge, but it must draw its own sustenance from the deeper wells of fascination and wonder. Thomas Berry, the "geo-logian" and Passionist priest, made an important point in this respect: one of the great tragedies of our degrading the natural world is that in doing so we are destroying the very source of our poetic and religious imagination. And in a vicious cycle, as the degraded world is less able to stir us beyond our intellect and ego, we are less moved to respect, preserve, or heal it. My children show me that beyond the world as we perceive it with our senses, scientific instruments, and five-year business plans lie realities far deeper than we can possibly conceive. That reality might be the "kingdom of heaven," which, as Jesus claimed, is already among us; it might be *Tir Nan Og* (the "Land of the Young") of Celtic mythology; it might be variously populated by fairies, elves, angels, energy, or quantum particles. Any of these is vastly superior to the "realistic" vision of so many developers and agribusinessmen, beneath which lies an unacknowledged mythological layer as well—namely, that profit is paramount. That myth has proven far more dangerous and destructive than any sort of more whimsical notions.

Realists—both those busy degrading the world and those trying to save it—would be better off if they learned once more how to play. The problem with the modern environmental movement is that, given the dire ecological state of the world and the apocalyptic attitudes of those of us with strong ecological concerns, stewardship of the land, as well as education and advocacy in the name of it, is generally undertaken as a Very Serious Business. One cannot blame people for such an attitude. After all, the survival of our species and many others depends on it! I cannot count how many earnest solicitation letters and e-mails I have received for a variety of environmental causes, which insist that my donation or action is the only thing that will head off utter disaster. Gloomy attitudes and doomsday predictions, unfortunately, do not make good advertisements for taking up ecological causes as a life-long discipline. But even beyond this marketing problem, the main issue with taking ourselves and our efforts so seriously is that we begin to believe that everything really is all up to us.

In light of the enormity of the challenges and the inevitable imperfection of our responses, calling out that the sky is falling inevitably leads to overwork, burnout, and despair—at least it does in my self-inflicted experience. Those who can stay faithful to healing work over the long haul are, ironically, those who have found a way to hold it a bit more loosely and to approach it with a certain degree of playfulness.

Not being particularly playful by nature, I am still trying to get the hang of play. Thankfully, my children are patient tutors. As a Christian, it helps when I recall that God is the author of all being and becoming, and that while we are called to cooperate with God, doing our part to bring our small, blue-green speck of Creation to its fulfillment, our part is but one of many. It is in God's hands, not ours, that Creation's fate ultimately rests. It helps also to keep in mind that the divine timeframe—to the extent that God relates to time at all—is infinitely longer than our own. We must, as the Jesuit priest Teilhard de Chardin urged, "trust in the slow work of God."

But while these insights from theology and cosmology may lessen my anxiety somewhat, it is from my children that I have learned what little I know about play. When melancholy and concern weigh heavily upon me, as they often do, my children have been a lifeline—especially Eli, who has brought exuberant, extroverted joy to our family of introverts. The kids' insistence on spending time with me, on dragging me away from the project at hand in order to play blocks or trains, go fishing, or skip rocks on our pond, has saved me again and again from the awful fate of being trapped in my own over-seriousness, which I know now is just a more publicly acceptable form of narcissism.

Laughter is often the password of this liberation and a gateway of divine revelation, as the playful Sufi poet Hafiz recognized in his poem, "Tripping Over Joy":

> What is the difference
> Between your experience of Existence
> And that of a saint?
> The saint knows
> That the spiritual path
> Is a sublime chess game with God
> And that the Beloved
> Has just made such a Fantastic Move
> That the saint is now continually
> Tripping over Joy
> And bursting out in Laughter
> And saying, "I Surrender!"

Whereas, my dear,
I am afraid you still think
You have a thousand serious moves.[1]

With so much of our past and present threaded with tragedy, pain, and evil, I must admit that laughter and wild abandon can feel disrespectful and insensitive. But I think true laughter is about something far deeper than escapism or mere entertainment. While not a scripture scholar, I nevertheless picture Jesus as having a healthy and even mischievous sense of humor, cracking jokes, making puns, poking fun at others, laughing wholeheartedly. In his poem "Manifesto: The Mad Farmer Liberation Front," even a sober writer like Wendell Berry recommends laughter in the face of societal and environmental woes, as a way to avoid being made into an unthinking automaton for government and corporations. "Laugh," he recommends. "Laughter is immeasurable."[2] Hafiz writes in another poem that laughter "is the glorious sound/ Of a soul waking up."[3] True laughter invites the humility of transcendence, when ego and agenda yield and we see things as they are: that our own lives are brief and limited, and that God's love and persuasive power are infinite.

In light of this, laughter helps us avoid taking ourselves, our beliefs, and our actions too seriously—a temptation that has done so much harm in religion, politics, and our relationship to Creation. At their young ages, our children laugh with a wonderful, silly, unselfconscious abandon. I would be cruel if I squelched it and a fool if I didn't learn to laugh along with them, for their sake and mine.

Though I have learned much from our children's curiosity, imagination, playfulness, and laughter, I think what most moves me about them is their vulnerability. From their utterly helpless first months to the sweet innocence of their early years, Cyndi and I have fretted and worried over them, trying to keep them safe, secure, and healthy. Once I was swinging Eva around by her feet in the front yard. As she screamed with pleasure and I spun around, I lost track of where I was. I did not realize until it was almost too late that our gyration had brought her head very close to a heavy plow that was parked on the edge of the yard. If I had been a bit closer and she had hit the plow, the impact would surely have killed her. That episode made me realize, though I try to not dwell on it, how quickly things can change—the freak diagnosis or accident, the random act of violence or other harm—and how limited our care and protection really is. Out of love we bring children into the world, and yet from their very conception their lives are subject to forces our love is impotent to predict or control. To be born means to enter into a web of freedom and chance whose consequences can be sublime or horrific.

As a parent I find this maddening, even though I know it is one of the ground rules of Creation. Modern science has demonstrated that the fundamental nature of existence is interdependence, which is another way of saying that everything is vulnerable to everything else—even things that seem imperturbably durable. Our planet is a tough old rock that has been around for billions of years, and yet it also hangs precariously in the void, a chance amalgam of cooled gases and recycled stardust upon whose roiling tectonic surface life, basking in the energy from the sun, has by some miracle emerged and thrived. The Earth and all forms of life upon it, including the human species, seem by turns obstinately durable and utterly fragile. Certainly the planet's thin skin of atmosphere, ocean, and soil have shown themselves especially vulnerable, not only to natural disaster but also to human meddling.

If the Christian tradition is to be believed, even God can be vulnerable. The Creator of the universe, who holds all things in being at every moment, chose to be made manifest in our world not as an all-powerful Lord demanding obeisance, but as a helpless little child in the arms of his mother. Jesus' brief life and ministry were about service rather than power. He was about conversion, not coercion, and so made himself vulnerable to rejection by his people and ultimately to execution by the Roman state.

Why? My experience among the poor and disabled at Holy Comforter in Atlanta and my life as a farmer, husband, and parent convince me that if we willingly embrace vulnerability in ourselves and others, we brush up against a profound, mysterious, paradoxical truth: that real power lies not in what is strong, impervious, and important, but what seems small, insignificant, and fragile. Real power is a love that accepts the authenticity of weakness and dependency, love that gives of itself even to the point of death, love that death and destruction cannot annihilate, love that after three days bursts forth with new life from a tomb that cannot contain it. Love is the only solid ground, the ultimate source of meaning and purpose in a universe marked by constant change, unpredictability, and the inevitable cycle of suffering, death, and rebirth. I cannot guarantee anything in our children's lives: that they will embrace our values, that they will inherit a habitable planet, that they will be safe, secure, or content. All I can do is love them with a strong hope that come what may, the mere fact of that love has added something good to the world. Love, our children teach me again and again, is what lasts.

chapter seven

Open Home, Open Heart: Hospitality and Belonging

I received no ticker tape parades for my efforts, but since returning home to make a life in Indiana, I have, for the most part, felt very welcome here. My mom and stepdad opened their home to me for several months, albeit with raised eyebrows, as I searched for a job and established myself on the land I had bought. St. Mary's parish and the community of Saint Meinrad welcomed me warmly into the strange, new world of Catholicism. From the first day John Schaeffer appeared in the field to help me fix my balky tractor to the countless other times when Paul Frey and many others have lent me tools, field equipment, labor, and expertise, I feel that the community of my rural neighborhood has made room for me. And though I have been a very imperfect tenant, I believe that even the land itself has welcomed me, inviting me to take up my place here in as gentle and loving a way as I can, bearing my missteps with a patient acceptance that comes from four and a half billion years of practice.

To some degree my family and I are still strangers in a strange land, and I suspect we will always be on the margins of conventionality. Having received such gifts of welcome in so many different ways, however, it is difficult to imagine not trying to extend hospitality to whomever and in whatever ways we can. This receiving and giving of welcome may well be the deepest root of our true belonging in this place, and even perhaps in the world at large. I realize that we are called to more than just creating a peaceable home; if we don't want to become insular and self-serving, we must open our home to others.

Whether to relieve guests from the rigor and danger of travel, to learn the latest news from afar, or to live out concretely the command to love thy neighbor, welcoming others has figured strongly for much of human history. Abraham and Sarah rushed to make a meal for the respite of their three visitors, who would leave them laughing with a strange promise of blessing. Jesus offered rest to all who were weary and heavy-laden. In the middle ages, monasteries became bastions of hospitality.

Many centuries later, hospitality remains one of the primary charisms of the monastic community of Saint Meinrad Archabbey. Its namesake, a somewhat obscure ninth-century Swiss monk, became known as the martyr of hospitality after welcoming into his mountain hermitage two thieves, who then beat him to death in order to steal whatever treasures visiting pilgrims may have left there. Long before this, however, St. Benedict had described in great detail the duty of monastics to open their doors to the stranger. "All guests who present themselves are to be welcomed as Christ," Benedict writes in Chapter 53 of his *Rule,* "for he himself will say: *I was a stranger and you welcomed me* (Mt 25:35)."[1] Later in that chapter he continues: "Great care and concern are to be shown in receiving poor people and pilgrims, because in them more particularly Christ is received."[2] Each year the Archabbey welcomes thousands of guests of various ages and backgrounds and religious inclinations. If Benedict is right, and my experience at Saint Meinrad confirms that he is, caring for these "pilgrims" is not merely an obligatory duty for the community living under his Rule. More profoundly, it is the opportunity to encounter the living God in the form of the stranger. In ways both strange and sublime, the guest is the bearer of revelation: where the new breaks through what is old, comfortable, and familiar.

Like the monastics, Cyndi and I have tried to make hospitality a core value of our household. Even when we were stuffed into the tiny barn apartment or living in our half-finished house with hardly a kitchen, we did our best to provide a warm welcome and a hot meal to various and sundry visitors. We had always planned on throwing a huge house-warming bash once I finished our house, inviting all the people who had helped us work on it. The house still is not entirely done, however—and probably won't be—so to my great regret, we still have not yet thrown that party. A friend of mine in Atlanta and his wife were unable to take a honeymoon when they first married, so they have been making up for it ever since, going on some small trip every year on their anniversary. Cyndi and I have done something similar, hosting the legions of our friends and neighbors in ones and twos and threes.

Cyndi has been the stalwart and steadfast anchor of our hospitality, for although I am good at inviting people and we both take pains to be present to our guests, the particulars of the welcome itself are largely her doing. Contending with a hopelessly sloppy husband, the chaotic messiness of three young children, and the grime and grit of life on a farm, with assiduous effort she keeps our house clean and inviting. She has become a masterful chef, crafting delicious meals from whatever is available from the gardens, the freezer, or the root cellar. An artist at heart, Cyndi is often frustrated at how little time she has had or made in recent years for painting, drawing, or sculpture. I truly believe and try often to convince her (with limited success) that at least for this period of her life, her creativity has found expression in the gentle, unobtrusive artfulness of her hospitality. Lacking such devoted skill myself, I honor it and marvel at it in her and in whomever else such qualities of welcome are so well honed. I can think of few higher callings.

Both of us have had some experience with living and working in intentional communities, and we have often toyed with the idea of whether for us, hospitality might not take the form of only inviting the occasional visitor, but of opening our home and our lives to others for the long haul, creating some sort of community on our farm. As an experiment to see how we liked living at close range with others (and to earn some extra income), once we vacated our barn apartment and moved into our house, we decided to rent out the apartment.

Over the past several years we have had a string of tenants who were graduate students at Saint Meinrad. Nick, a young man from Connecticut, kept largely to himself but has stayed in touch, often mentioning that his year on the farm with us was a really important time for him. Casey, divorced and in her early 60s, stuffed the apartment with a collection of spinning wheels in various sizes, taught Cyndi how to knit, and became another grandmother for our children. Chris, just out of college, became an intimate part of our domestic life. He often joined us for meals, helped out on the farm, played with our children, carpooled with me to Saint Meinrad, and played guitar with me at our local parish.

Even with our various guests, however, living in a sparsely populated area has meant that most of the people we encounter are familiar to us in one way or another, or share somewhat similar convictions, education levels, or socio-economic circumstances. We have welcomed several people who are somewhat strange, but few who are strangers. In that sense, I have often feared that our rural farm is not so different from a gated residential "community" in a suburb, or any other area designed to keep the real stranger at bay. As with our settled life in general, I have found myself wondering whether even our household hospitality can settle into a pattern of predictability, in which we don't believe or expect we will encounter anything new (In ten years, we haven't even had a trick or treater!). Cyndi and I often ask ourselves whether we might be called to some more radical form of discipleship.

As we ponder this, I have also considered if one step toward a deeper sort of welcome might be to pay closer attention to the guests who seem so familiar to us, and discover ever-new aspects in them. As I have learned in getting to know Cyndi through our married life, even (or especially) those with whom we are most intimate can surprise us on a daily basis. When Eva and Clare turned one, my mother was diagnosed with an incurable form of non-Hodgkin's lymphoma. Although five years later she is doing remarkably well and is practically asymptomatic, this sword of Damocles serves as a constant reminder to me not to take her presence in our lives for granted. I am convinced that if I could learn to look with fresh eyes, I would begin to see all of our guests, and perhaps every person I meet, as a deep well of mystery, a complex amalgam of experiences, ideas, opinions, desires, and motivations out of whose depths some new thing can always emerge. Every person, even those as familiar as our close family, could become a revelatory stranger who would enter not only into our home, but into the often-locked fortress of our own well-worn thoughts and prejudices.

For that matter, I could encounter myself as a revelation-bearing stranger, cultivating openness not only to others, but also to what is mysterious in myself. Even after years of "inner work" in the form of spiritual direction, counseling, journaling, and introspective prayer, I realize that there is much about myself that I do not understand (or even particularly like), but which hospitality nonetheless bids me to explore and accept. Why, for example, do I have such a strong need to appear competent and in control? Having realized this need, my temptation is to whip and condemn myself for it. What would it look like if, instead, I tried to welcome this part of me as I would a guest in our home? I suspect that real, lasting personal change would stem from just this sort of open-hearted acceptance — again and again and again — rather than browbeating. Even if it didn't, I still think that I would rather err on the side of kindness and gentleness, to myself as to a guest.

Living on a farm, in close relationship to the natural world, I am learning that hospitality extends beyond the outer and inner realms of the human. Just as our land has welcomed my family, we are trying likewise to show welcome to the plants, creatures, and seasons of this place. We do our best to tend the health of the soil, creating hospitable growing conditions for our crops. We have welcomed stray pets; made a home for livestock; and come to know the owls, raccoons, coyotes, fox, deer, wild turkeys, rabbits, and other wild creatures that inhabit or visit this place. Of necessity, we have come to accept the heat and humidity of summer, the dreary cold of winter, the gentle cool of fall, and springs that are by turns lovely and stormy. Mindful of our environmental footprint, we are trying to live in such a way that the world will continue to be a welcoming place for future generations of plants, animals, and people, and that the distinct seasons of our region will continue to roll predictably on, one into the next.

Hospitality, then, means far more than just welcoming other people into our home. I have come to see it as a wide-reaching spiritual practice, which invites me to notice, welcome, and accept, well, *everything*. Every person, every experience, every moment is a God-given opportunity to encounter and learn something new and so be changed by it. Hospitality bids me to cultivate not only an open home, but an open heart, which is expansive enough to welcome Christ in the form of whatever new thing presents itself. If it is true that everything in the universe is interconnected and that everything somehow relates and belongs to everything else, then there is nothing, no matter how distant or disconnected in time or space from my direct experience, that does not deserve my care and concern.

Of course, I won't claim for a moment that such a broad understanding of hospitality, or our family's practice of it, has resulted in consistent feelings of oceanic oneness with the universe. Hospitality might be about an open home and an open heart, but homes can be shut and locked to keep out both weather and intruders, and hearts can be grievously wounded without some care and caution in their exposure. The world is a marvelous place indeed, but also a difficult and dangerous place—both in the wildness of the natural world, and in the wildness of humanity—what theologians might call fallen humanity. Though for very different reasons, both nature and human beings alike can be unkind, and sometimes we open our door at our peril. Many a night while camping, hearing the scuffle of a nearby bear or the howling of wolves, I would have wished for better protection than the flimsy walls of my tent. Even on our farm, where we have tried to cultivate openness to everyone and everything, we are very glad that the coyotes live in the woods rather than our living room. With no desire to be martyred like St. Meinrad, Cyndi and I would exercise prudence before we opened our doors to just anyone. Hospitality has its limits.

There is much to be said for healthy boundaries, but there is no denying that in a world where the unfamiliar can be threatening and terrifying, true hospitality is not just a healthy spiritual practice, but at times a fierce, difficult, and even dangerous discipline. Meinrad the saint faced the ultimate test of hospitality when he welcomed in those he knew (like any good clairvoyant saint) would slay him. In Atlanta, after seminary I moved into a basement apartment in the parish center at Holy Comforter, and at all hours various wild characters would knock at my door. I always marveled at an intentional Christian community I got to know in Atlanta, aptly named The Open Door, which has as the core of its mission a commitment to welcome all who struggle with drug or alcohol addiction, homelessness, and plain-and-simple misfortune. L'Arche, The Catholic Worker, and many other communities and organizations likewise open their doors to people who are not always easy guests. Not far from our farm, I know a family who, already having several healthy children of their own, felt convicted to adopt a baby girl with profound mental disabilities. This girl, they were told, would never be able to perform even basic functions on her own. Raised with loving care, she recently graduated high school.

I am humbled by such radical hospitality. I believe authors like Jean Vanier, Henri Nouwen, and Dorothy Day are right that the welcoming of challenging guests can be the locus of profound encounter and revelation. But this is *hard*: full of discomfort and messiness. I want an ordered, neatly organized life and a clean, well-lighted dwelling place: everything (even the guest) under my control. Opening myself to that which is unpleasant or threatening, or even just weak and full of need, reminds me yet again—uncomfortably—of my own vulnerability, weakness, and need.

And yet however I might eschew them, I know it is through these cracks in my carefully constructed veneer that God can enter my life in a truly meaningful and transformative way, instead of serving as mere window dressing of a house otherwise in order by my own power. As much as I want to appear strong and "together," in my more truthful moments I know that God is less interested in congratulating the spiritually accomplished than in welcoming, holding, and healing those who realize and accept their own brokenness. Jesus spent his time among the sick and wounded and disgraced, and he had few kind words for those who saw themselves as morally pure and religiously impeccable. "My grace is sufficient for you," Christ assured St. Paul, "for my power is made perfect in weakness." "When I am weak," Paul then asserts, "then I am strong" (2 Cor 12:9–10).

What a different message than the popular culture's ideals of imperturbable strength, energy, control, and competence, or the perverted "prosperity gospel" circulating among some Christians, which conflates material wealth and success with God's favor and blessing. Hospitality is often difficult, and hospitality often fails. In America, which so highly prizes the individual, I'm not sure that the fibers of the social fabric have ever been especially strong. And if one receives no welcome, it is difficult to extend welcome to others; the life of the community suffers, and the possibility for true belonging recedes. Though Cyndi and I always find ourselves wishing for more connections to our immediate community, we are very fortunate for the degree of welcome we have found in our local parish, our rural neighborhood, and the unique community of monks, faculty, students, and staff at Saint Meinrad. I know it could have been different, and in many places, with many people, it is. How much genuine welcome can one expect in a depressed urban slum, rife with poverty and violent crime, or at the other extreme, in an enclave of relative prosperity, especially if one's income and connections are not quite up to snuff? How much welcome does one receive as an unskilled, illegal immigrant; as a gay or lesbian; as a Republican among Democrats or vice versa; as a woman in male-dominated cultures; as a refugee of Sudan, Iraq, or other desperate and dangerous regions?

Or what happens when welcome is offered but refused because of pride, prejudice, injury, insult, or just mere busyness? A few years ago a middle-aged couple, Mike and Brenda, built a house on property immediately east of our farm. We aren't friends or natural companions, and our lives do not intersect a great deal, but we have become good neighbors, entering into the exchange of casual chat, favors, and equipment that defines many rural relationships.

To our north, however, a young man recently took up residence in a run-down farmhouse. Due to both his and our reticence, almost a year passed before we even learned his name—the learning of which has been about the extent of our dealings with him. On his part and ours, neighborhood hospitality has failed, which I remember every time I resent him as he and his friends roar by at breakneck speed in his souped-up pickup truck or mufflerless ATV.

Whether on the scale of neighborhood or international relations, whether in regard to human beings or ecological concerns for the present and the future, the failure of hospitality stands as yet another ready reminder of the stubborn persistence of sin and the great need of salvation. The whole Creation, St. Paul so wisely perceived, is groaning for redemption. My own heart is groaning; my family members are groaning; the abused soil and decimated wild creatures on and around our farm are groaning; those in my community and far beyond it are groaning; the whole earth is groaning; the beautiful and terrifying cosmos as a whole is groaning. We were created to welcome and be welcomed, to belong fully and deeply in this wonderful world, and yet that belonging is ever marred and imperfect. We belong, and yet we don't. Any alteration of that stark truth will require a power far greater than our own.

chapter eight

Simplicity, Sacrifice, and the Struggle to Stay Put

Ten years into this homesteading experiment and finally in a position to reflect more intentionally on it, I recognize a recurring set of challenges in our attempt at crafting a sane, simple, and faithful home. Although I intended to live very simply, I have discovered that the "simple life" of my dreams is, in reality, exceedingly (though wonderfully) complex. Our convictions about simplicity have often meant making sacrifices, which I have come to see as something far more meaningful than a strongly principled stoicism. One of those sacrifices has been staying in this particular place and this fairly predictable life, a commitment that has led me to wrestle with the strange angels of restlessness and resentment. From my own experience as well as from the Benedictine tradition and the monks at Saint Meinrad, I have learned that the hidden gift in these challenges is the doors they open, again and again, to prayerful attention, gratitude, and ever-deeper conversion.

145

Simplicity and Complexity

"Our lives are frittered away by detail," wrote Henry David Thoreau in reflecting on his famous two-year experiment with simple living at Walden Pond. "Simplify! Simplify!" I admire Thoreau, and in many ways *Walden* has been both a motivation and a measure for the life I have chosen, but I also understand that ours are two different projects: he was a young, single man roughing it for a short while on borrowed land in an earlier era, while I am trying to create a long-term, sustainable life with a family, on our own land, in a century whose complicated realities (and virtual realities) would have likely made Thoreau drop his hoe and flee to Antarctica.

In the age of Facebook, Twitter, cell phones, itemized tax deductions, and health insurance paperwork, I'm not sure that the simple life is really possible any more, unless the definition of "simple" is stretched and contorted into something hardly recognizable. Cyndi and I have been intentional about trying to keep our family's life focused on essential things, but I know all too well that the term "simple" probably isn't a fair descriptor of what we have achieved. "Simpler" is closer to the truth: simpler than it would be if we *weren't* mindful, and simpler than the culture of consumption has encouraged (at least perhaps until the bottom fell out of our economy), but even so, far more complicated than I had ever imagined or hoped. We have long since given up my fanatical, perfectionist, self-righteous ideals of total independence and sustainability, opting instead to acknowledge our compromised complicity in the sins of a complex age, and now work toward a more realistic, humble, and compassionate form of "rugged interdependence."

Much of what makes simplicity such a difficult endeavor in the Western world comes from powers and principalities far beyond my power to control or even understand. I have little to say about the political machinations in Washington, even if the laws that result from them impact my day-to-day existence. I have only a vague understanding of complex credit default swaps and mortgage-backed securities, but the global economic collapse they helped create has changed my life and the life of everyone I know.

Even in the more human-scaled realm of the home, complexity is unavoidable. One can certainly scale back and de-clutter, forgoing the extra car (or for some, any car), the second home, the satellite TV, the job that pays well but entails stress and long hours, the endless extracurricular activities, the attic or basement full of unused and unneeded junk, even the cell phone—all of those things that often cause more headache than satisfaction. But even if one purged those things, just meeting basic needs is still no simple matter. I have often joked that a simple home economy would be working a job with little challenge or responsibility, living in an apartment, and eating every meal at McDonald's: a life in which, as long as I got my paycheck and paid my bills, I could remain happily ignorant of all that provides my shelter, water, food, and energy. While this kind of life would be simple for me, however, it would just kick the can down the road, using the money I earn to farm out all of the complex processes that support my existence. When it comes down to it, merely staying alive is a complicated business.

From an ecological perspective, then, the kind of simplicity Cyndi and I try to pursue is an ongoing attempt to reduce our needs, simplify those that remain, and in many cases reclaim more direct responsibility for them ourselves. It is easy enough to eat at a restaurant or even to buy food from the grocery without considering the long, fragile, wasteful supply chains that brought it there. It is far more complicated to raise one's own food or to buy it from local farmers, even though in the final analysis that is generally a simpler and more sustainable choice. It is easy enough to adjust the dial on a thermostat and to write a check to the utility company every month, forgetting that in most cases, warming one's house ultimately warms and degrades the planet, as well. It is far more complicated to manage the harvesting and burning of firewood or the design and construction of a sun-heated home.

I had the naïve notion that eschewing the rat race would mean that I would have more time to cultivate intellectual and spiritual concerns while doing the hard but satisfying physical work of supporting our household needs. I have found, instead, that the complex demands of simplicity often end up being in tension with my desire to nurture the less tangible elements of a creative and faithful life. Over the last decade, I could have said many more prayers, read many more books, made much more love, gotten much more sleep, and enjoyed many more evenings with friends and family in the time I've spent building, tending fields and gardens, repairing equipment, making firewood, and the myriad other chores of our household economy. And though I may have avoided various distractions, such as TV or video games, I have certainly spent a lot of mental energy preoccupied with vexing practical problems instead of more "spiritual" ones. Often I resent how complicated and challenging the simpler life in fact is, and I find myself wondering if the thousands upon thousands of hours I've devoted to various mundane tasks have dulled my brain and my spirit rather than sharpened them. Would it be better, perhaps, to work less and pray more?

I think my frustration has come from assuming a certain exclusivity and competition between the practical arts of doing and making required in a healthy and intentional home, on one hand, and the less tangible pursuits of learning, cultivating relationships, and prayer and worship, on the other. Because we are physical creatures in a physical world, matter matters, and even the most devoted devotee still has to eat, drink, and stay clothed and warm. *Someone* has to provide for those needs, and unless we believe in a spiritual hierarchy in which the mundane many support the holy few, at least part of our time will be invested simply in maintaining our physical existence. Is this really just wasted time, to be minimized as much as possible—often through exploiting cheap labor or natural resources, in order to tend the "better part"? Didn't Jesus praise the contemplative Mary and admonish the busy and distracted Martha?

The forty-eighth chapter of the *Rule of Benedict* reflects on "the daily work." In this chapter, Benedict discusses in specific detail how monks are to order their day, making time for personal contemplation and reading, communal prayer and liturgies—and manual labor, for "when they live by the labor of their hands . . . then they are really monks." Benedict advised monastics to strike a balance between *ora et labora*, prayer and work. Prayer was to take precedence, but work and physical needs were not to be devalued: even the tools and goods of the monastery were to be handled, he stresses in chapter 31, "as sacred vessels of the altar."

With only so much time in a day, I suspect I'll always feel some degree of competition between the time I spend attending to material needs and the time I devote to prayer, being with loved ones, and cultivating other qualities of a good life. But if Benedict is right about the importance of labor and the tools of labor, even in the life of an individual whose entire life is given over to prayer, then the competition must not be absolute, nor the two realms entirely distinct. Living artfully must mean not only seeking an ever-changing balance between action and contemplation, but also trying to meld the two realms whenever possible. I would like to believe that a healthy home economy can mirror monastic principles: that it is possible, and in fact necessary, for the good work of maintaining one's practical needs also to nurture the more sublime concerns.

In my experience, household work can be prayerful and meditative, if approached in the right way; it can be an activity that draws people together with laughter and love and common purpose; it can be the occasion of meaningful, stimulating conversation. In my better moments, I have bonded deeply with my family and friends as we have picked strawberries or folded clothes, and I have had contemplative experiences and said heartfelt prayers to the pounding rhythm of a splitting maul or the drone of my tractor. On my less banner days, however, I have fled to my work as an escape from the messy challenges of my family life, or resented solitary chores because they drew me away when I would have rather spent time with others, with a good book, or on my prayer cushion. Home economics as a spiritual discipline means, then, finding a way to make the unavoidable work it entails into prayer, even as one tries to balance work and formal prayer with the other goods of a well-lived life.

I have found no set formula for this other than the constant effort to carve out some time each day specifically for prayer, and to try to infuse all activities with a prayerful attentiveness. I no longer believe that there is a static end goal or fixed picture of what this looks like, for like everyone, my circumstances and inclinations are always evolving. Because seasons dictate much of my family's life circumstances, I pray and work differently in the busy growing season than I do in the dark, quiet months of winter. And, of course, at all times I experience the blessed interruptions of our young children, who both shatter my attention and invite me into a deeper form of it. Remaining faithful to prayer and work requires constant recalibration and a profound trust that God, full of patience and good humor, continues to draw me closer through the myriad ways in which I stumble, fall, and fail at it.

Simplicity and Sacrifice

Simplicity, as we try to embody it on our farm, entails not only openness to complexity, but sacrifice. Much of recent talk about climate crisis and ecological stewardship centers on the idea that clever technology and efficient use of resources will end up ensuring humanity's future, all the while preserving the Western standard of living and bringing developing nations up to this standard. I do believe technology and efficiency are important, and I certainly believe that billions in poorer nations deserve a far better existence than they have. Given the limits of natural resources and a growing population, however, I strongly suspect that it will be impossible to navigate toward a socially and ecologically sustainable future without personal and communal sacrifice from those of us in wealthy countries.

Perhaps the day will come when we will be forced, ready or not, into some apocalyptic, Darwinian struggle for survival, such as many of the world's poorest face even now. For my part, I would rather freely and consciously choose a simpler life that entails sacrifice than be thrown into it (or fear being thrown into it) by some ecological, economic, or social collapse. I see such a choice as an expression of solidarity with those who are impoverished. It is also an attempt at justice, simplifying my needs so as not to take more than my fair share of the earth's resources. And much like athletic training, sacrifice is a way of "toughening up," preparing for a less prodigal lifestyle by tangible and concrete actions that begin to embody it in incremental steps, right now. Seen from a spiritual perspective, giving up some conveniences and comforts and taking on the hard, complicated work of a simpler life is really a new form of asceticism: eco-asceticism, if you will.

Asceticism has a rich history within the Christian tradition as a spiritual path. The early monastics took to the Egyptian desert because they perceived that there, in tough circumstances, they could peel away distractions and come to the core of their own selves and life itself. The desert was not for the faint of heart: it imposed on these zealous seekers a radical asceticism, simply to survive. Like the desert monastics, my family and I have come to accept—sometimes joyfully, sometimes grudgingly—that our attempts to live more simply and justly will entail a certain degree of inconvenience, discomfort, and self-denial. Asceticism, in other words, involves discipline: physical, mental, and spiritual. At their best, the desert monastics disciplined their minds and bodies not out of self-loathing or to strut their ego, but in fact to rid themselves of themselves: to die to their small ego-self and discover beneath and beyond it a True Self that, as Thomas Merton realized, lives in union with the Divine and with the essence of all things.

Even with my family's efforts to live more simply, I realize that, relatively speaking, our privilege is vast and our asceticism rather tame. One of our "eco-ascetic" disciplines, for example, is to forego air-conditioning so that a little less coal gets ripped out of a strip mine in Montana or a blown-off mountaintop in Appalachia, and a little less carbon dioxide warms up our global greenhouse. Such a choice is certainly no great act of heroism or creativity. Plenty of folks on this planet do it every day, in much worse conditions, and *all* of us did it for most of human history. Small as this sacrifice may be, though, it still feels like sacrifice. I don't *like* to be hot, to sweat through my clothes, to spend hot afternoons and evenings fighting heat-induced torpor, desperate for a breeze from weather or fan. My wife was raised on a farm in Pennsylvania, without air conditioning, and she bears it better than I, who grew up in a suburban house with painted-shut windows, where the turn of season in spring and fall meant simply moving the thermostat switch between "heat" and "cool." So on some hot days I just steam, in resentment and discomfort. As with

Lenten fasting, these days invite *kenosis*, or self-emptying, after the model of Christ, who as St. Paul wrote in the letter to the Philippians, could have had all but chose less. In these times, I am trying to look at sacrifice not so much as a form of teeth-gritting for a higher purpose but as an opportunity to realize that my discomfort and my resentment need not have the final word. They are just one more thing to notice and then let go, giving them to God's safekeeping.

Ego-charged willpower for self-deprivation, then, is precisely *not* what healthy eco-asceticism fosters. This is partly because any spiritual practice is a false path when it serves primarily to enlarge the ego (like the proud Pharisee bragging about his prayer, fasting, and almsgiving) rather than helping one discover the much larger True Self that transcends the individual ego. But mostly it is because, at least in my experience, ascetic sacrifice for the sake of ecological and social concern is generally a source not of misery, but of pleasure and satisfaction. Certainly, I enjoy the somewhat abstract benefits of saved money and a (somewhat) assuaged environmental conscience. As importantly, though, I have found what a relief it is to be a little less dependent on technology, at least in this one small regard. My family and I have been encouraged by the realization that we don't *need* air-conditioning to survive the summer. We are tougher than we thought, and our house, while sometimes uncomfortably hot and humid, is livable.

When I am not busy resenting the discomfort, I can even say that I enjoy going without air conditioning, because doing so helps tear down the sense of separation that it and almost all technology tends to create between me and the world in which I belong. My understanding of Catholic sacramentality and the theology of the incarnation (the mystery of God becoming human) is that true spiritual practice brings you closer to the tangible world rather than further from it; so does turning off the AC and opening the windows! This helps you begin to savor your surroundings, for when you open the windows, your senses open, too. When you are hot, you notice any small shift of breeze, slight drop of temperature or humidity, or blessed rain shower.

If you live out of eco-asceticism long enough, you begin to notice the cycle of the day, from pleasant mornings to brutal afternoons to merciful evenings after dusk. You notice your own blessed body as it works to maintain its own equilibrium as best it can in the circumstances. On our farm, open windows allow us to hear the birds heralding the morning, the thrum of cicadas and the chorus of bullfrogs singing into the night, the throb of field equipment, and the ongoing neighborhood symphony of dogs, goats, cows, coyotes, and roosters. And yes, we also smell the manure I just spread on the fields, and the skunk that frequents our place at night.

As the sacrifice of conveniences and comforts removes some of the barriers between me and the world around me, it is teaching me to pay attention. With deep, sustained attention to the world, it is impossible not to feel awed by it, grateful for its many gifts, moved by the suffering with which it is rife, and in all this, aware of our marvelous belonging in it—even as we prepare for a yet fuller belonging in the world to come. In some sense, then, toughness and strength are mere by-products of simplicity and sacrifice. The real spiritual fruit is a softer, more expansive heart, which is open, aware, grateful, and compassionate: a heart in harmony with the wide reaches of God's sorrow and God's love.

The Struggles of Staying Put

I committed to a "vocation of location" on a farm out of a belief that loving, faithful stewardship to a particular place, aside from being necessary in terms of planetary finitude and health, could be a journey of discovery far more exciting than the restless wandering (geographical and otherwise) that our culture holds up as an ideal. Benedictine monks take a vow of stability, by which they commit to spend their lives in one place, with one community. After a decade of working with and befriending many monks of Saint Meinrad, I have come to see how this vow is really a simple invitation to journey toward outer and inner authenticity: to work beyond surface impressions or pretensions to a more transparent, deeper sort of belonging to themselves, their community, and their place.

The truthfulness that comes from stability, however, almost always comes at a cost. As filled as my life has been with the varied challenges of farming, building, family life, and rewarding work in the field of ministry formation, I must admit that I have often wondered, with a certain degree of weariness, whether its various rhythms have become ruts. "Is this all there is?" I have found myself asking: these same neighbors, friends, colleagues and family members, this endless round of going to work, doing laundry, changing diapers, planting and weeding and harvesting, repairing old equipment to make it run another day? Does what I'm doing truly make any significant difference, or is it simply self-serving? While I believe that our life is a good one, and while my love for it runs deep, at various times that love falters and dims.

When the early Christian desert monks struggled with soul-numbing boredom, doubt, discontent, and restlessness, Abba Moses, one of the wise monastic voices from this period, famously counseled: "Go, sit in your cell, and your cell will teach you everything." In other words, the monks were not to flee to the distractions of another place or even the life of the community, but rather to confront it head on in the very solitude that was its genesis. I still find Abba Moses' advice a helpful reminder of how useless it is to flee from my own inner demons, either by seeking out some other home or more favorable set of life circumstances, or by distracting myself from them with frivolous pursuits, such as watching television, or even worthwhile ones, such as helping others. I know I would bring my demons with me to whatever new place or activity I sought out, and when they set up shop, what appeared a greener pasture from afar would soon seem similarly bland.

Surely there are toxic situations where it is necessary simply to abandon ship for the sake of survival. And even in the best of circumstances, some time away can bring much-needed perspective and restoration. Otherwise, I believe that remaining in one's "cell"—which as Ronald Rohlheiser has pointed out, is simply another name for the place, circumstances, and responsibilities that can seem so oppressive and stultifying—provides the only true way forward. It means staying put and confronting the demons by taking an honest, introspective look at the *why* behind my boredom.

Other than perhaps the broad idea of "original sin," I won't speculate about any universal sources for human discontentment. Everyone has his or her own baggage, and I am expert only regarding my own. What I know from my own experience is that a deep look inside can be a painful revelation. When I enter into silence and solitude, I often encounter a howling cacophony of interior voices; of anger, fear, and anxiety; of plans and projects and other chattering distractions. These, not the externals of my situation, I suspect are the real causes of my lassitude. They constrain my vision into myopia, making me see only the shortcomings of my chosen life.

My monastic friends and colleagues have taught me that the life of faith has a kind of trajectory: conversion, which is in fact one of the primary vows Benedictines take. Building a faithful home is indeed a ceaselessly spinning wheel of life with all of its repeating tasks and seasons, but the wheel is meant to roll *somewhere*: toward greater virtue and virtue's divine source, even if we will never reach perfect beatitude this side of heaven. Building a faithful home, like God's grace, offers me again and again the opportunity of conversion: the chance to turn away from my self-preoccupation and toward the needs of other people and the good work I have been given to do. Such as it is, my own conversion has rarely occurred in dramatic moments of catharsis, but in the daily choices I make regarding the small and seemingly trivial tasks of our family's home economy.

Do I choose to wash dishes with boredom, resentment, and the distractions of external and internal noise, or with true attention and gratitude for the gifts the washing embodies: a good meal just eaten, a body healthy and well-fed, the sensual pleasure of warm water on my skin? I don't always manage to do small things with great love, as Mother Teresa recommended. Sometimes the best I can do is a plea (often after the fact!) that God forgive and make good out of the scattered restlessness of my mind, heart, and will. The grace, I think, is to keep trying.

Conversion is not just the journey of inner growth and being fitted for eternal life, but also a process of learning about and responding to the tangible physical world I occupy. Just as sacrifice can lead to greater attention to the world, so also is stability an ongoing invitation to discover the best way to inhabit a place. I used to think, foolishly, that I would somehow arrive at the perfectly calibrated life here on this farm: that after years of hard work I would get everything in place, just so, and the rest would just be ongoing maintenance. But having put in those years of hard work and settled fully into this life, I know now that were such an ideal even possible, it would be a static life and therefore not life at all, but a sort of living death.

In reality, beyond my boredom and internal discontents, I am coming to see that there is always something new to learn about dwelling in this place, this lovely, living laboratory. I am ever experimenting with new ways to farm, learning from books, from others' advice, and mostly from my own mistakes and failures. And I am constantly dancing with the inevitable, often weather-related disasters, such as a recent ice storm that devastated many trees on our property. In all this, I try to keep in mind Wendell Berry's maxim: the most important products of a farm are not what is sold off it, but the health of the soil and the improvement of the farmer's mind and character—and, I would add, the quality of his or her relationships.

Like enlightenment in the Buddhist tradition, true conversion that results from fidelity to one's place and one's responsibilities in that place turns one outward toward the world and engenders a compassion that fuels active, fruitful, world-repairing work: the Jewish idea of *tikkun olam*, or "perfecting the world." A tree bears fruit through its instinctive fidelity: by standing still, putting down roots, and stretching its limbs to the sky. I believe that any real human fidelity—choosing to attend truthfully to a place, a community, a spouse, a vocation—brings a similar blessing of fecundity, which is meant to be shared as a healing gift for the world. For at its core, the real power of fidelity is not duty or principle or moral uprightness or even truth in the abstract sense, but love, which Saint Paul knew to be the deepest truth of all: "The greatest of all these is love." And love, by its very divine nature, is wildly and wonderfully generous.

God calls us to love and make our home in Creation, and out of our truthful fidelity to places, relationships, and good work within both, God promises us the gift of fruitfulness, whether it be children, a productive farm, a creative pursuit, a strong community, a healthy civic life, or an expansion of the inner frontier of faith and wisdom. I believe God calls everyone to be faithful,

fruitful lovers, whose love adds something precious and beautiful
to the world.

Conclusion:
Home-Grown Hope

For my family and me, choosing the life we have has meant foregoing much of what would pass for success in the United States today. We have a modest income with some money in the bank but little extra. We forego various luxuries, conveniences, and creature comforts. We take upon ourselves the responsibility of providing the heat, water, and much of the food and energy our household requires. To do this means that we do a lot of grunt work, and that we don't have a great deal of what most would call leisure.

At times I brood about everything we have given up and all that we have taken on. But most of the time, I look on our life as one of utmost privilege and satisfaction. Most of what we lack we don't really want anyway, and the responsibilities and tasks to which we have given ourselves provide us with soul-deep satisfactions that no amount of wealth could purchase. Though our life in this place has been a choice (or rather, an ongoing series of choices), I harbor no illusions that we have created it out of sheer willpower and mental resolve. By almost every measure, our life is a gift for which I can thank God, but which also results from the happy fortune of having a good education and job, physical and mental health, political stability and religious freedom, some financial capital, and a supportive network of friends and family. It could have been different, and I am all too aware that for the vast majority of the world's population, especially in developing nations, it is: such a combination of resources is tragically out of reach. And so in the midst of our household satisfactions, I struggle with a great amount of guilt. We work hard, but we also experience much happiness and fulfillment, which feels almost blasphemous in the face of so much suffering and misery the world over.

I struggle also because I know that our privilege has come at a price—a price borne by disadvantaged peoples and by animals, plants, climate, and soil, both now and in the future. Though we have tried hard to live gently and reduce our environmental footprint, it is still sizeable. We still run gallon upon gallon of fossil fuel through our vehicles and farm equipment; we still own a great deal of stuff (much of it made by people who are underpaid and exploited); constructing our house required a great deal of resources. We, too, have a part in forests felled, wars waged for oil, lands desiccated and denuded, the climate changed, and landfills stuffed with toxic refuse . . . to a lesser degree, I hope, than if we were not intentional about our choices, but still to an extent that makes me despair of our household economy ever being anything like sustainable and just.

Short of reverting to a hard-scrabble existence bereft of comfort, leisure, or pleasure—and who would go for that if they could avoid it?—I am not even all that sure what a sustainable individual life or a sustainable community would look like in its particulars. My ideal of a durable, resilient economy would be that most of a region's food, energy, and other basic necessities would be produced locally and on a small scale, in a diverse landscape that has its own unique character, from carefully stewarded, renewable resources whose use results in no unusable or toxic waste products, by skilled people who are invested in their work and their place. Communities would accommodate the unique needs and gifts of individual members, and all people, especially those in urban vis-à-vis rural settings, would realize their mutual interdependence.

While I'm dreaming, the lion would lie down with the lamb, too; I know this is an idyllic vision. So many things would have to change in our culture and economy to reify it that I have little idea how society as a whole might move toward it. I fear we might never embody it enough, and soon enough, to avoid dooming ourselves and countless other species to extinction. Even supposing we do shift our priorities, it seems clear that with much irreversible damage already done, we can anticipate a more crowded planet; a warmer, weirder climate; and degraded ecosystems that will need a long time to heal.

I do believe in the basic goodness of people and of the world, but I am not so naïve as to think we can simply innovate or legislate our way out of our current ecological and social predicaments. The fault lines of sin run too deeply through each one of us and through all of our civic and economic institutions. All of us are wounded and carrying heavy burdens, and almost all individual and communal endeavors are an ambiguous combination of love and apathy, humility and arrogance, courage and cowardice. And even if sin and brokenness were not in play, ignorance bears its own destructive force. In an exceedingly complex, interconnected world, even well-intentioned actions often have unforeseen consequences that defy the predictions of imperfect human knowledge and foresight. On the grand scale, who could have predicted global warming and the ozone hole? In my own family, how could I have known that a thoughtless word or action would so infuriate my wife or wound my children?

I struggle, finally, to reconcile myself to the radical impermanence of human life and Creation as a whole. Even the enduring authors and poets leave their marks for centuries or a few millennia, a mere blip on the scope of human evolution, much less cosmic history. My family and I, whose lives and work will likely be far less memorable, will probably be forgotten far more quickly. I could invest my life in the improvement of our farm, only to have my work undone by the carelessness of subsequent generations: poor farming, "development," war, nuclear weapons, or radical climatic change.

Even if this land (along with the rest of the planet) is stewarded well by those who come after, as I hope and pray it will be, such kindly treatment cannot halt the rise and fall of oceans, the advance and retreat of glaciers, the bump and grind of tectonic plates, the explosions of volcanoes, or the impact of a stray asteroid or meteor. It certainly cannot forestall the entire planet's eventual destruction by the spending of our sun, and I am not so optimistic that by such time the human race—on the outside chance that it still exists at all—will have cleverly transplanted itself to some other planet. Everything is transient, as the Buddhist tradition has recognized so clearly, and the earth itself will wear out "like a garment" (Is 51:6). Ultimately, Creation alone offers no truly solid ground.

Home-Grown Hope

In the face of these struggles, and the anxiety they often cause me, I wonder constantly: what hope can ground my life and give it purpose and direction? My life and my efforts are miniscule and fragile relative to the needs of this planet, the vastness of space and time, and the creative and destructive powers of the universe at large. In the face of this sobering truth, I can think of only two real options: either my life is utterly meaningless and insignificant, or else it is infinitely precious and valuable in some mysterious way I cannot fully fathom. If the former is true, then I suppose I could soldier on as a brave stoic and try to live with uprightness and generosity though I see no final sense in it. Or I could seek only my own pleasure with no concern for others, or even kill myself in existentialist despair.

Perhaps I'm just not courageous enough for stoicism or suicide, or audacious enough for blatant selfishness, but I cast my vote on the side of hope and meaning. I refuse to believe that the care and concern I feel for my family, for the human race, and for all of Creation are simply delusions with which I comfort myself, or my genes trying desperately to ensure their continuance. For me, hope is an absolutely essential ingredient of survival, and I choose to believe that there is good reason for hope—even if I don't understand the mysterious depths (or heights) from which hope springs. To the best of my limited abilities, I try to live out of that belief.

I have no instruction manual for exactly how to do that, either for myself or for anyone else. I am still barely able to articulate the questions, much less any answers, of what it means to hope. Even knowing so little, however, I do realize (as I mentioned at the beginning of this narrative) that I am rather unmoved by abstract or large-scale assurances of hope, be they theological, political, environmental, or economic. If my life on this farm has shown me anything, it is that for hope to have any real consequential impact on my life, it has to be home-grown: discovered and cultivated in the everyday rhythms of a faithful, responsible, authentic, and even joyful household economy.

As Wendell Berry once pointed out to me in a kind but steely tone, hope is a discipline. Like love, hope is born and developed in the gritty reality of daily circumstances; it must be chosen anew, over and over again. And like love, I believe that the discipline of hope is a gift. On my own strength, I do not possess the virtue and willpower required to keep choosing hope, but through my relationships with others and with the Creation, I fancy that God keeps encouraging and empowering me to make that repeated choice.

In my life, home-grown hope has emerged out of my efforts, however small and stumbling, to do good work that I can believe in: befriending and tending the small patch of Creation that is our farm; fostering quality ministry formation for the students in Saint Meinrad's programs; or using music, writing, and other creative means to offer something beautiful to the world. Hope has emerged in the wonderful, difficult push-and-pull of relating to my wife and children, my extended family, my colleagues at Saint Meinrad, and others whose friendship is dear to me. It has emerged in successes and failures Cyndi and I have experienced in our attempts to reach out to the community of our rural neighborhood and our parish, receiving and offering hospitality through the sharing of our gifts and of our need.

The hopefulness I have sought and found in all of this has less to do with the outcomes of my efforts and more to do with the experiences themselves and the quality of heart and mind with which I try to approach them. I am unable to explain exactly how, but I simply *know*, deep in my bones, that it is good and right to split firewood, to work in the gardens with my family, to welcome others into our home, and to build relationships with customers at farmers' markets.

I hope that my family's home economy does indeed make the world better, but I also realize how little control I have about how things turn out on either the small scale or the large. Even the best-laid plans can end in disaster, and I could die tomorrow, or this afternoon, with much left unfinished. So in some paradoxical

way, faithful home economics means both working toward meaningful goals—in my family's case, a fertile farm, smaller environmental footprint, and healthy relationships—and at the same time,
becoming less attached to the end result of my efforts, focusing
instead on what I happen to be doing in any given moment. With
what intentions do I hoe the row, relate to my wife, praise or discipline my children, invest my talents in our parish or my work
in ministry formation? Does my ego run the show, with all of its
baggage and brokenness, or can I be freed from the ego enough to
notice how the sacred shines through at every moment, whatever I
might be doing? Can I find a way to honor the past and enable the
future by being fully here in the present?

I no longer believe, as I once did, that a hopeful life would
result from attaining some state of perfect enlightenment in the
spiritual plane and sustainability in the ecological. Both of those
continue to elude me, not only because of my own limitations and
weakness, but also because it is impossible for one individual living in a broken world to achieve a perfectly healthy life that con-
tributes nothing to the world's brokenness or is unaffected by it.
Creation is one, in the sublime and in the suffering; we rise and
fall together. For me as a Christian, the Cross of Christ stands in
the middle of this conundrum. The Cross puts the kibosh on any
naïvely optimistic notions that the human race will, with just the
right laws and motivations, finally get its act together. The Cross
speaks a different message: that reality shows little mercy to the
idealist, that pain is threaded through every fiber of existence, and
that God turns the human categories of "success" and "failure" or
"weakness" and "strength" on their heads. All roads lead to Calvary; no one gets out unscathed. The question is not whether we
can defeat or even simply avoid suffering, because we cannot, but
whether we can face suffering with a faithful hope.

That hope, for anyone who has faith in a loving God, claims that redemption, not suffering, is the final word. I believe that by some unfathomable means, God is drawing the Creation toward some presently unimaginable end in which all that is broken is healed, in which all pain and suffering—throughout all time—find both relief and resolution, in which all that seems meaningless makes sense, in which all that seems wasted is restored, in which all that is separate comes finally to a full and rightful belonging. As a Christian, I see a foreshadowing of that redemption in the resurrection of Jesus. As a farmer, I see it in the spring flush of new green on my abused fields. As a husband, I see it in the reconciliation that follows a fight with my spouse. As a father, I see it in the dried eyes and tentative smile of my upset daughter or son. Though I have no idea when or how a final redemption will occur, I see enough glimpses of it to know that I want to live toward that redemption, with all my heart and soul and strength, in whatever ways I can.

I find myself, then, on a journey of discovery: growing (I hope) in knowledge, wisdom, and generosity; and learning how to form and sustain authentic relationships with other people, with the rest of Creation, and finally, with the Creator. My Benedictine friends would call it a journey of conversion, whose goal is to become more and more like Christ; I think Wendell Berry would call it "traveling at home." Trying to live with home-grown hope means embracing the strange paradox of an intense commitment to my particular place in the world, but also a belief that in a material world as tempestuous and transient as ours, we are all pilgrims whose final home both includes and lies somewhere beyond the world of our five senses. Perhaps that world is "heaven" or "eternal life," whatever those seemingly worn-out words might mean. All I know—all I *need* to know at this point—is that whatever redeemed world is to come, the only bridge to it is from *this* world:

this blessed, broken, beautiful world, which is so worthy of love and care. Hope takes root here and now, where the small, humble work in the place we call home points the way to a much larger home, where everyone and everything belongs.

Acknowledgments

A ny worthwhile book—like any worthwhile life—emerges out of community and gratitude. While I leave it to readers to decide the merits of this book, I know without a doubt that it and the life it describes have been made possible by a great "cloud of witnesses" who have inspired me, worked with me, put up with me, and been amazingly generous to me. These few words can't possibly convey how grateful I am, but as with all imperfect language, I hope they point the way.

My wife Cyndi, of course, deserves far more thanks than I can ever muster, and probably more than I even realize. Foolish and brave enough to marry someone as quirky and driven as I am, she has been muse, critic, fellow dreamer, and partner in love and in work. She has been a patient, gracious, grounding force in our household, a marvelous mother for our children, and a quiet, profound voice of wisdom and sanity. I hope to be even half the husband that she deserves.

Fr. Guerric DeBona, O.S.B., a monk of Saint Meinrad Archabbey and one of my closest friends and colleagues, has shown me by word and example what it can look like to be both authentically human and deeply faithful—to God, to a place, to a community, and to a vocation. He, along with Sr. Patty Lasher, O.S.B., encouraged me to write when I bemoaned the lack of any time or courage to do it. A skilled writer himself, for several years he has been the first reader and merciless, challenging editor of almost everything I've written. For his friendship, for his example, and for his inexhaustible help, good humor, and good counsel, I cannot thank him enough.

Patrick McGowan, my editor at Ave Maria Press, has been everything one could hope for in an editor. He and Ave Maria took a chance on a young and new writer, and throughout this process, Patrick has been unafraid to challenge me, and quick to support and affirm me. Without his convictions and his keen eye, this book would have ended up grumpier, more judgmental, and less true. Patrick's careful and courageous editing has made this a better book and me a better writer—but more importantly, a better human being. I am grateful.

Many to whom I owe much appear in the preceding chapters. Others have gone nameless or unmentioned, not for lack of influence, but for lack of space. For the steadfast support of my parents, even amid head-scratching, I am thankful to Joyse and Nelson Rivers, and Tom Kramer, and to the vast community of their and my friends and relatives. I have learned much about honest, open vulnerability in the face of great suffering from my friend Fr. Joe Weigman. To Fr. Drew Christiansen, S.J., and the staff of *America* magazine, I am grateful for the wonderful privilege of adding my voice to the public square of ideas. To Fr. Joe Merkt, who introduced me to Cyndi and has been a fine friend and counselor to us both, I owe an unpayable debt. Our neighbors Paul and Becky Frey, Eric and Jenny Schmidt, Jack and Marianne Schriefer, among others, have invited me into a belonging I scarcely deserve but to which I hope to live up.

Our children Eva, Clare, and Elijah are the reason I wrote this book. When I forget what gratitude, laughter, or wonder feel like, they remind me. It is out of hope for them and the world they will inherit that I try to live rightly and to teach them the joyful challenge of good stewardship.

Finally, one of the central characters in this book is not a human being at all, but still deserves grateful mention. Genesis Organic Farm, the land I have called home for ten years, has been my mentor and measure and muse, a visible sacrament of God's patient, redeeming love. Though the legal papers say that the land belongs to Cyndi and me, the real truth is that we belong to it— and together, we all belong to God.

Notes

Chapter Three: Loneliness and Love

1. Wendell Berry, *That Distant Land: The Collected Stories* (San Francisco: Counterpoint, 2004), 284–5.

Chapter Five: Farming and Food

1. Michael Pollan, "Unhappy Meals," The *New York Times,* 28 January 2007, Magazine Section.

Chapter Six: Children at Play

1. Daniel Ladinsky, *I Heard God Laughing: Poems of Hope and Joy* (New York: Penguin, 2006), 66.
2. Wendell Berry, *Collected Poems 1957–1982* (New York: North Point Press, 1984), 152.
3. Ladinsky, *I Heard God,* 65.

Chapter Seven: Open Home, Open Heart: Hospitality and Belonging

1. Timothy Fry, O.S.B., Ed., *The Rule of St. Benedict 1980* (Collegeville, MN: The Liturgical Press, 1981), 255–7.
2. Ibid., 259.

Kyle T. Kramer is a writer, farmer, and lay ministry program director. He is the founder of Genesis Organic Farm in Spencer County, Indiana, and the director of lay degree programs at Saint Meinrad Archabbey, a Benedictine monastery, seminary, and graduate school of theology in southern Indiana. Since early 2009, Kramer has been a regular contributor to *America* magazine. He holds an MDiv from Emory University and serves as vice president of the Association of Graduate Programs in Ministry and as a regional leader in the National Association for Lay Ministry.

Founded in 1865, Ave Maria Press,
a ministry of the Congregation of
Holy Cross, is a Catholic publishing
company that serves the spiritual and
formative needs of the Church and its
schools, institutions, and ministers;
Christian individuals and families; and
others seeking spiritual nourishment.

For a complete listing of titles from

Ave Maria Press

Sorin Books

Forest of Peace

Christian Classics

visit www.avemariapress.com

ave maria press® / Notre Dame, IN 46556
A Ministry of the Indiana Province of Holy Cross